Starting and Running a

GASTROPUB

or BRASSERIE

Location,
financing,
pricing,
marketing,
designing,
equipping,
menus,
staffing &
accounting

Carol Godsmark

howto**books**

D1386336

Published by How To Books Ltd,
Spring Hill House, Spring Hill Road,
Begbroke, Oxford OX5 1RX, United Kingdom
Tel: (01865) 375794 Fax: (01865) 379162
info@howtobooks.co.uk
www.howtobooks.co.uk

First edition 2007

British Library Cataloguing in Publication Data
A catalogue record for this book is available from
the British Library.

ISBN: 978 1 84528 201 1

Produced for How To Books by Deer Park Productions, Tavistock
Typeset by *specialist* publishing services ltd, Montgomery
Cover design by Baseline Arts Ltd
Printed and bound by Bell & Bain Ltd, Glasgow

Note: The material contained in this book is set out in good
faith for general guidance and no liability can be accepted
for loss or expense incurred as a result of relying in particular
circumstances on statements made in the book. The laws and
regulations are complex and liable to change, and readers should
check the current position with the relevant authorities before
making personal arrangements.

Starting and Running a Successful
GASTROPUB
or BRASSERIE

Contents

City College Norwich

Customer name: MR James Brackley
Customer ID: 1784**

Title: Food and beverage management. (4th ed.)
ID: A216336
Due: 09 Jan 2012

Total items: 1
28/11/2011 14:26
Checked out: 3
Overdue: 0
Hold requests: 0
Ready for pickup: 0

Thank you for using the
3M SelfCheck™ System.

Preface

How to get into today's most popular eating-out businesses

Starting and running a gastropub or brasserie, today's two rising stars in the eating-out business, is an aspiration of many. You may be weighing up the pros and cons of entering this vibrant business and being your own boss. You may be thinking of a career change: would-be restaurateurs come from a wide range of backgrounds and fulfil their ambitions via these two relatively more relaxed restaurant types.

You can share in this growth market.

This book will guide you through the pitfalls of starting up your business in this rapidly developing restaurant sector. You may wish, as many do, to take a lease on a pub and transform it into a gastropub, or you may consider buying a country or urban pub. You may prefer to go down the brasserie route and buy an existing business or set up one that reflects your own personality.

A growing number of pub and restaurant diners are demanding more information about where their food is sourced. This applies particularly to gastropubs and brasseries which have taken the lead in this initiative. This is key to the business, so a great interest in food provenance is required, local and regional ingredients becoming essential for your menu. Stephen Bull, proprietor of *The Hole in The Wall*, Little Wilbraham, Cambridgeshire and one of the great chefs of his generation believes that, 'good food in pubs is obviously the future. Pubs are a relatively cheap way for ambitious, decent chefs to start on their own because of the low outgoings and the social environment that many chefs find congenial.'

People increasingly want to eat freshly-prepared food to counteract the soulless fast-food business and you can share in this, be it in a gastropub or brasserie.

Many people dream of ditching the nine to five job and entering a world of creativity and hospitality. There are those, however, who naïvely see it as a way of making a fast buck, with customers flowing through the doors on day one without very much effort on the part of the new restaurateur. Realism is an essential ingredient for any business, and this is particularly true in the field of hospitality as it involves so many aspects of life: people, location, food, drink, legislation and long hours.

Restaurants are part of the hospitality and entertainment business, but it is a tough business. It is also a most rewarding, stimulating one, both on a personal level and a financial one if it is approached and run with prudence, professionalism, control, dedication and a dash of imagination and flair. And you have to like people.

As a restaurant journalist, critic and chef (I am also a restaurant consultant, guide inspector and past chef/restaurateur) I have researched and written this book from an experienced, practical base. This vital book will guide you through the steps needed to achieve a viable business.

I'll explain clearly and in depth everything you need to know about:

◆ the history of the gastropub and brasserie and definitions of both types of businesses;

◆ running your own gastropub or brasserie, and your required strengths and personality;

◆ your location, property scrutiny and legal requirements;

◆ financing your business;

◆ book-keeping, accountancy and pricing;

◆ marketing your business;

◆ designing and equipping your business;

◆ running a safe, hygienic business;

◆ designing your menus;

◆ choosing beer, wine, coffee and other drinks.

I'll also tell you:

◆ how to choose food suppliers and specialist food and equipment suppliers;

◆ how to staff a well-run premises;

◆ how to deal with customer relations and about being a customer;

◆ how to solve business problems;

◆ how to approach the day-to-day running of your business.

This book will help you put yourself in your customers' shoes and guide you to building up a loyal trade. It is written with the novice restaurateur in mind and is also invaluable for those already in the business who may wish to trade up to meet current customer expectations.

It includes useful trade addresses and a whole host of top tips throughout the book, all based on the experiences of accomplished chefs, restaurateurs, suppliers and others in the profession.

If your passion for running a gastropub or brasserie takes hold, I wish you every success and fulfilment in one of the oldest, most rewarding businesses in the world.

> *The British public's growing appetite for dining out is matched only by the hunger of wheeling and dealing in the restaurant scene by buyers and sellers. Mintel reports a 5% rise in eating out with £28 billions' worth of meals consumed in Britain last year.*

Please note that for the sake of brevity the terms 'gastropub' and 'brasserie' are collectively described as 'restaurants' in the book.

1

What is a gastropub?
What is a brasserie?

In this chapter I introduce you to the twin phenomena of gastropubs and brasseries, as well as suggesting you take a look at your own strengths in relation to running one of these establishments. I cover your motivations and expectations as well as must-have attributes and those of any partner you take on board.

The new British dining institutions

The gastropub

Goodbye to the old boozer, hello to civilised eating and drinking in gastropubs and brasseries. The gastropub, Britain's very own version of the French *bistro* or *brasserie* or the Spanish *tapas* bar has at last come of age. Confident and influential, the gastropub movement has grown into a vibrant and essential part of all that is good about British food, cooking, style and hospitality in the 21st century.

Drawing on influences from Britain and Europe, the gastropub repertoire and style of business is now increasingly to be found in all parts of Britain. However, it appears in many guises, some the genuine article, others far removed from the model that makes it truly appealing. Ideally, it offers seasonal, fairly priced, unpretentious, home-cooked food, this newly created platform launching some of the country's most talented and energetic chefs keen on cooking more informal food.

Not that long ago pubs had an image problem regarding food – pub meals were frequently appalling affairs with the likes of curly-edged, bendy, white bread sandwiches, inferior pork pies and leathery, fatty sausages. Less than 30 years ago, fewer than 10% of London's pubs sold hot food. Now that figure is 90% even if some of the food is pre-cooked and microwaved.

Gastropubs are breeding. 'The gastropub phenomenon is showing no signs of slowing down,' says Derek Bulmer, the *Michelin Eating Out in Pubs 2007 Guide* editor. Among its 559 entries, there are 48 in London alone. Gordon Ramsay opened his first gastropub in London in 2007 and plans a substantial number of country gastropubs as well. Jean Christophe Novelli plans ten around London, and Marco Pierre White has already opened one in Berkshire, *The Yew Tree Inn*, near Newbury, although he prefers the term 'eating house'. Increasingly gastropubs have letting rooms too: another lucrative string to their bows.

According to Mr Bulmer, 'the general public want that flexibility and informality', the emergence of these culinary pubs banishing the likes of scampi in a basket. 'Ten years ago there was not a chance of a high-profile chef working in a pub,' he says, 'a lot now are going back to their roots and getting a lease on a pub.'

Gastropubs, progressively more popular in the South East, are also spreading to all parts of Britain as publicans, chefs and entrepreneurs seek to cash in on this lucrative market for high-quality local food. Customers often prefer the overall experience of a typical gastropub to that of almost any restaurant.

A Restaurant Association spokesman says that 'pubs are ideal for chefs who want to try their own thing. They already have an infrastructure in place so it's just a case of utilising what's there instead of all the overheads of opening a brand new restaurant.' This is exactly what business partners who are credited with the creation of the movement did.

During the 1980s recession, struggling breweries became increasingly keen to offload the leases on under-patronised, urban pub sites. Business partners Mike Belben and David Eyre took a brave gamble in 1992 when they acquired *The Eagle* in London's then unfashionable Farringdon Road, one such declining pub. Keen to open a restaurant, but lacking the necessary finance, they embarked on a project that swiftly became the blueprint for the new generation of gastropubs. Although they dislike the term, it nevertheless is shorthand to describe this type of pub-restaurant. Belben and Eyre are always cited as opening the first gastropub. But they were beaten by Paul Clerehugh who opened *The Crooked Billet* in Stoke Row, Henley on Thames in 1990. Today, it retains the unspoilt rustic country charm that made it famous, its large and varied, daily-changing menu specialising in local and British produce. Buffalo milk and honey ice-cream are sourced from a buffalo farm next door and Paul's own bees, whilst beef, lamb, hogget and mutton come from Paul's farm. A blackboard on the front door encourages guests to swap their home grown delicacies for lunch.

Although recognisably pubs, the new school brings much more than just a wide range of bottled beers to attract clientele. Offering real food instead of merely salty fuel, booze is no longer their sole *raison d'être*. Often airy, user-friendly and with nice, big, clean windows you can actually see through from the street, these new British watering holes also ensure, thanks to their more egalitarian style, that women no longer 'need a lot of bottle' to walk into a pub.

Increasingly these days, pub closures by the big breweries can often mean a takeover by chefs and/or entrepreneurs new to the trade; the pub reopening with an open kitchen where the darts alley used to be. Stripped pine floors, old school tables and chairs are standard, as is the badly written blackboard with its menu on view: the handwritten menu a no-no here. Customers can eat at more reasonable prices, the atmosphere is casual to, frankly, laidback in the extreme. It is extraordinary how quickly the gastropub concept evolved from a radical invention to a burgeoning high street or village staple.

Egon Ronay, the *Egon Ronay Guide* editor, reports that the emergence of gastropubs is the biggest change in British catering over the last half century. 'They often produce food of restaurant standards despite having "cramped" kitchens and overburdened cooks,' the guide says.

Describing the emergence of gastropubs, Mr Ronay says: 'Though around for some time they are a phenomenon having spread explosively with a surprisingly high standard of cooking and warm-hearted atmosphere – altogether the biggest change in the catering scene in my fifty years' experience as a restaurateur and critic.'

But there are dissenters. Some gastropubs are just restaurants in a pub framework, places where the bar has shrunk and having a pint with crisps or a sandwich isn't really an option,' says Stephen Bull of *The Hole in the Wall*, Cambridgeshire. Marco Pierre White of *The Yew Tree Inn*, near Newbury, suggests involving the whole community 'as long as they are polite and friendly', and his 'eating house' takes on local people as much as possible. Derek Bulmer of the *Michelin Eating Out in Pubs 2007* warns that 'some city chefs are trying to replicate restaurant menus, but this doesn't necessarily work, bangers and mash still being one hallmark of a good gastropub.'

The gastropub bandwagon continues to roll, with new venues opening up each week. The smoking ban is having a huge impact on pubs in general; the food continuing to take precedence over the pint, a smoke and a packet of crisps. 'This will change the whole face of the pub world,' Marco Pierre White predicts, with more pubs turning into gastropubs to attract customers.

Typical British-type food to be found in gastropubs may include home-made soups, pressed gammon terrine with home-made pickle, potted shrimps, Lancashire hotpot, roast pork belly, braised lamb shank, venison burger, rib of beef, salmon fishcakes, pot roast chicken, wild mushroom risotto, hand cut chips, crumbles, cheesecakes and tarts. Bar snacks are being pushed out, the sandwich not profitable enough.

The brasserie

The brasserie is also coming of age in Britain. Originally the personification of simple French *bistro*-type food served in classical *fin de siècle* surroundings by long-aproned waiters, the brasserie differs from the gastropub in style and type of food; the emphasis on more refined, yet simple, food and décor. If you want a full-blown meal like steak and *frites* in the middle of the afternoon, you need a brasserie. Croissant and coffee at nine? Tea with pastries at four? Tarragon chicken salad or eggs Benedict at 11 pm? Head for the brasserie.

Bridging the divide between the formality of the restaurant and the coffee-and-sandwich option of a café, brasseries offer a more relaxed approach to eating out alongside the gastropub. But not at the expense of the food.

The word 'brasserie' comes from the French *brasser*, meaning, 'to brew'. Brasseries, early in 19th-century France, were originally small informal restaurants attached to breweries serving beer, wine and simple food. They developed into more elaborate restaurants than cafés or bistros, usually open long hours with a limited menu available throughout the day.

Brasseries came into prominence after the war of 1870 when many Alsatians fled to Paris to escape the German occupation of their homeland. The establishments they opened were elegant and ornately decorated. *Bofinger*, *Brasserie Flo*, *La Coupole* and *Au Pied de Cochon* were some well-known ones which are still going strong, despite changes in French society's needs.

Brasserie St Quentin, one of the first real brasseries in London and now in its 26th year, is a prime example of the best in *la cuisine bourgeoise*, sourcing quality produce from suppliers and farmers around the country and abroad. The hallmark of *St Quentin* is simple: classic dishes made from the best ingredients at an affordable price.

Typical brasserie dishes may include *coq au vin*, *canard a l'orange*, *daube* of beef, trout with almonds, omelette Arnold Bennett, *foie gras* and chicken liver *parfait*, oysters, salads, steak *tartare*, rib steak and *frites*, *choucroute garni a L'Alsacienne* and *crème brulée*, available all day. These dishes plus *croissants*, full English breakfasts and porridge are found at *The Wolseley*, Piccadilly, the grandest of brasseries in the UK and which is open from 7 am to midnight.

Both gastropubs and brasseries differ from mine-host pubs where drinking is often their prime *raison d'être*, with perhaps an area given over to tables for meals. However, these are changing, too, as eating out is becoming the norm rather than the exception with one in three of us taking the financial plunge once a week, or more. But many pubs, particularly chains like *Wetherspoons*, rely on processed food to serve to their customers, unlike the gastropubs and brasseries whose first priority is mostly good food cooked on the premises from carefully-sourced ingredients in relaxed, unfussy surroundings. Gastropubs and brasseries are often the best choices for a lazy, lingering weekend brunch, newspapers thoughtfully provided by some management.

Becoming a restaurateur

Becoming a restaurateur either in the UK or taking the plunge abroad is a fantasy many people have. But, in reality, the thought is put on the back burner due to a lack of knowledge on how to proceed. Or could it be the cold feet symptom: the leap from being an employee to being self-employed is simply too daunting?

As an employee, your work might be unrewarding, unstimulating and predictable. Or you may be locked into a profession that no longer inspires. You may long to develop a creative business you feel you have strengths in; the restaurant world having always attracted you.

Is being in a partnership with family members appealing, the urge to control your own destiny a motivating factor? Could you work with a friend who has agreed to enter into partnership with you?

Being a good chef can be just the catalyst some people need to chuck in the day job and open a restaurant, their partners perhaps also agreeing to the new venture by throwing in the corporate towel, too. But are you a good enough cook to sustain the business week in, week out? Or could you be a good front of house manager/business partner, being able to offer not only excellent hospitality but managing staff, the accounts and the ordering as well as dealing with customers?

The good news is that more and more people are eating out with the gratifying result of a mushrooming of restaurants to suit every culinary whim – as demonstrated by the successful numbers of gastropubs and brasseries opening. The bad news is that this business is not suited to all, even those with strong aspirations to own and run a restaurant.

Your restaurant will reflect your personality

What kind of a restaurateur do you see yourself as? A restaurateur who offers acceptable food and is in the business purely as a money-making venture? Or a restaurateur who sees the trade as a way of life, and seeks to change and mature as well as explore new ideas whilst learning from other chefs and restaurateurs? But who also, through judicious management, stays afloat financially?

What type of restaurant appeals to you most? A gastropub or brasserie? Explore the market to see where you would like to be – town or country – and what the competition is like. See the chapter on location for further research.

If you see your business as just a bit of fun or purely as a money-making venture, think again. It takes skill, dedication, hard work, long hours, an ability to sell your business to the public, enthusiasm and loads of energy and commitment. Being a restaurateur is a hard, unrelenting, competitive way of life, but it can be immensely satisfying, rewarding, pleasurable, entertaining, intense and stimulating. If you find the right market and are good at what you do, you will make a good living. And it is certainly never dull!

Should you decide to join this way of life, you will be entering one of the oldest professions in the world, one that is very much part of our lives in all cultures. Pure theatre.

Working out your strengths

The concept of being your own boss is very energising, but it is worth analysing your personality, skills and strengths and those of others who are entering the business with you, both professionally and personally to see if you – and they – have the necessary attributes.

These questions need to be answered honestly. You will need the majority of these qualities to run a successful business. What do you do well? What are you skilled at? Hopefully you will find that a number of your skills can be used to run your own restaurant.

This analytical list is not meant to put you off, but to help you become more aware of the skills it takes. If many of the answers are in your favour, other attributes will be gained along the way.

◆ Are you fed up with your job and looking for a change in lifestyle?
◆ Do you want to be your own boss and keep the profits?
◆ Are you really positive about creating a new business?
◆ Are you motivated, organised and self-disciplined?
◆ Do you have good business sense?
◆ Do you have the ability to remain calm under pressure, thrive in chaos?
◆ Are you flexible? Can you think on your feet? Are you a problem-solver?
◆ Are you creative? Able to infuse a little creativity into all parts of your business (and I don't mean tax creativity here!)?

7

◆ Are you a leader, a communicator? You'll be dealing with all kinds of people.

◆ Are you competitive?

◆ Are you efficient?

◆ Do you have a good grasp of how food is produced?

◆ Have you taken on board the fact that you will be saying goodbye to a secure pay packet and fringe benefits for the time being?

◆ Have you the money to gamble, knowing you are taking a risk?

◆ Can you take advice? Learn new skills?

◆ Can you cope with increased stress levels?

◆ Do you have good health? (You need to be reasonably fit and healthy to run a gastropub/brasserie as the work is labour-intensive with long hours.)

◆ Do you have a warm personality, a hospitable nature?

◆ How do you really feel about the service industry?

◆ Is your goal realistic and attainable?

◆ Most of all, do you like people? If you find dealing with people on many levels a trial, then running a restaurant might not be for you.

You'll also need to consider the following issues:

◆ Examine what skills you possess, where you may have weaknesses and what you can do to overcome them.

◆ As your busiest period is weekends, you will need to ask yourself how this tallies with family life. Is your family committed to this change of lifestyle and will they back you wholeheartedly?

◆ Bear in mind, too, that it may be a long haul before the business is successful – you and your business partners, should you have any, will have to share the ups and downs and have the right temperament for the hospitality business.

◆ You must be confident enough to sell your business plan to banks, customers and the media, and to take advice and learn new skills.

◆ Learning how to delegate and prioritise will also be invaluable, as well as having the stamina to work long hours.

Don't be put off by this lengthy list. Not all the questions will apply to you as you may have partners, colleagues and staff who might be able to fulfil some of these roles required for running a successful venture.

While you read this book and think about running a restaurant, bear in mind that things won't be perfect from day one. Even several years down the line things always need improving. You will learn through trial and error, as most new businesses do, while you gain experience on a daily basis.

> *For some, becoming a restaurateur is like being given the keys to a sweet shop, aka, the booze cupboard. Alcohol can be the downfall of a restaurateur as, per capita, no industry drinks more than the restaurant one. Handling drink is a high priority.*

2

Gastropub or brasserie?

This chapter tackles the pros of running either a gastropub or brasserie, with some insights into both by owners and managers. As the British public – in common with trends in the Western world – are eating out more and more, the types and styles of restaurants have diversified to meet demand; hence the rise in popularity of the gastropub and brasserie.

The gastropub

Gastropubs are taking on the restaurant trade both in town and country with customers flocking to them in their droves. And why? They have developed into a fully-fledged dining institution with all the cosiness and neighbourliness of a local pub that serves mainly modern, gutsy British food at (for the most part) reasonable prices. This reinvention of the traditional pub is driven by talented chefs determined to show that food doesn't have to be formal to be fabulous. Chefs are using locally-sourced ingredients to create memorable food and serving it in an unforced and unpretentious atmosphere.

Repeat business is guaranteed if the place has the right feel and the right food, a good selection of wines by the glass and bottle and decent on-tap local beers. And, it goes without saying, good, knowledgeable, friendly staff are essential in any hospitality business.

Thirty-one per cent of pubs are independently owned, with the proportion set to rise as brewers and pub companies sell off unprofitable sites to chefs, restaurateurs, tenanted publicans and others looking to run their own businesses. Bankers, city traders, entire families and business investors are buying or leasing pubs with many head chefs and second chefs taking the plunge to be more in control of their lives. Older pubs in city centres or in villages are highly sought-after.

The smoking ban in enclosed public places came into force in Wales in April, 2007 with England following suit in July of the same year. It is predicted that families and others who dislike eating in a smoky atmosphere will gravitate towards eating in pubs as they are seen as a safe, now healthier – and informal – option. The smoking ban was introduced in Scotland in March 2006. Punch, Britain's largest pub landlord with more than 9,200 pubs, has commented that Scottish customers very quickly appreciated non-smoking pubs.

As publicans are no longer likely to make a profit on wet sales alone, food has become the saving grace, another pointer to the success of the gastropub.

General economic factors, such as increased disposable income, low unemployment rates and the increase in dual income families, have resulted in a booming eating-out culture. Gastropubs are likely to attract people not used to eating out whilst those already choosing them are more likely to become regulars but, if prices are too close to more upmarket restaurants, once-appreciative diners may desert them. There is a danger of the concept being taken over by giant pub chains with their lack of culinary skills in the kitchen, giving a bad name to the sector.

Owner/manager viewpoint

Marco Pierre White, the youngest chef to win three coveted Michelin stars, and now businessman, opened *The Yew Tree Inn* near Newbury, Berkshire, in 2006 as an 'eating house, not a gastropub', the term representing for him one of 'false representation about food'.

Nevertheless, this pub with rooms is where he involves the community by either offering employment or a pub meal of excellence: the menu a cornucopia of roasts, grills, egg dishes, fish and seafood. He also shoots and fishes locally for the larder. A drinking area to encourage locals is on the cards, as currently they have to negotiate diners and rather upmarket artefacts that reflect this fine-dining chef's past.

Gareth MacDonald McAinsh, *The Yew Tree*'s manager, believes that in ten years' time most pubs will be like this, with good food the norm and with a relaxed atmosphere. The resolutely Anglo-French menu is seasonal and with none of the fashionable ingredients like *pak choi* or balsamic vinegar. Nor are they looking for a Michelin star as it would do more harm than good, alienating locals and destination diners alike, he believes. However, other gastropubs such as *The Stagg Inn*, Herefordshire and *The Star* at Harome, Yorkshire, have Michelin stars and have only benefited from them.

The gastropub look

The gastropub look runs from the eccentric (mirror screens at *The Yew Tree Inn*, tablecloths, napkin rings) to the more typical with bare floorboards, worn furniture, mismatched chairs and tables, soft couches around an open fire, wooden bar, oak beams, separate dining rooms in some and the must-have hard-to-read blackboards with rubbed out items. Some are quite ramshackle as shabby chic is currently fashionable.

The brasserie

Peter Langan is credited with the re-emergence of the brasserie in the UK with the opening of *Langan's Brasserie* off Piccadilly, London in the 1970s. The large, bustling brasserie with its walls covered in fine art and its haphazard selection of lampshades, has an Anglo-French menu and was an instant hit. Brasseries are where people like to be seen, *Langan's* is no exception.

Brasserie St Quentin rivals *Langan's Brasserie* for longevity. Other brasseries opened in London, but very few took off elsewhere in Britain at the time. Terence Conran, one of Britain's most prolific restaurateurs, followed suit with the *Bluebird Brasserie* in the King's Road, London and *Café Boheme* opening in Soho in 1992. It serves brasserie food from 8 am to 3 am, with live music from 4 pm.

Café Rouge, the rather soulless chain, started operating in 1989 and imitates what the owners think a typical French bar-café-brasserie should look be like. Now its 80 restaurants in the Tragus Holdings empire have been joined by another small chain, *L'Abbaye*, Belgian brasseries.

The daddy of them all, *The Wolseley*, on Piccadilly, opened its flamboyant doors on the site of the Wolseley car showroom in 2003 and is the epitome of the sector. Jeremy King and Chris Corbin, two exceptional restaurateurs responsible for *The Ivy*, *Caprice* and other London restaurants, were looking to emulate the *grand café* experience where the public could have the option of breakfast, coffee, brunch, lunch, afternoon tea, drinks and dinner or late supper: all bar the traditional French onion soup at midnight or dawn. Their biggest influence was Peter Langan. *The Wolseley* was an instant success, a true blueprint of continental brasseries, and also taking inspiration from Viennese cafés as well as Parisian brasseries like *Les Deux Magots* and *Café Flo*.

Sam's Brasserie, Chiswick, London, opened in 2005 and is part of the newer look in brasseries with a modern interior in a former paper factory; the menu, however, is traditional brasserie-style.

Owners' viewpoint

Brasseries are egalitarian, with duchesses sitting next to taxi drivers, according to owners. They are meeting places with relaxed informality and usually situated on a main street for convenience. The space should have a magic for people to want to go there and feel as if they are on holiday. Generally, there are reserved tables but some keep back tables (around 30%) for walk-ins. They often offer magazines, newspapers and some even offer shoe-cleaning and Internet facilities. Some are able to have outdoor seating to evoke even more of a sense of Paris.

The brasserie look

Some, like *The Wolseley*, *Langan's* and *Baltazar* in New York demonstrate a *fin de siècle* Parisian feel with aged mirrors, paintings, banquettes, long bars and lamps in a grand space. These brasseries go for tablecloths, long white-aproned waiters or ones wearing black short aprons with black waistcoats and white shirts. Windows are generally uncurtained to allow the public to see in and diners to see out with, perhaps, a half Parisian curtain which still allows for a view of the street.

Less traditional brasseries like *Sam's Brasserie* are ultra-modern in look with bare tables, mirrors and modern paintings on the walls, red banquettes and leather seating.

3

How do I get into the business?

This chapter covers the first steps to consider for entry into the restaurant business via sole trading, joint partnerships or forming a limited company. It also guides you on how to approach buying an existing business or becoming a partner in an existing business.

Whatever your background, you'll first need to consider how to get into the business. There are four possible ways to becoming a restaurateur:

1. Buying or leasing a property, starting it from scratch and developing it slowly, but surely.
2. Buying an existing business with premises, equipment, staff and a regular customer base with a good name and reputation.
3. Becoming an investment working-partner in an existing business.
4. Working for an existing business with well-respected professionals to learn about it with a view to becoming a partner.

But first, consider whether you will go it alone, take partners or form a limited company.

Being a sole/joint trader

The definition of a sole trader is that the business is owned and operated by one person. If two people join forces it is known as a partnership. A sole trader, whether or not in partnership, is personally liable for debts.

Advantages

◆ A sole trader business is easier to set up with fewer formalities and legal constraints than a partnership or company.

◆ There is no need to share the profits with anyone other than your agreed partner(s).

◆ A sole trader has complete control over the business, the direction it is heading, the style of the food, expenditure, marketing, etc.

◆ There is no one to answer to as there would be in a partnership or company.

Disadvantages

◆ If not in a partnership, you are the only boss and, as such, can find it difficult to get away at all, let alone to have a holiday.

◆ You are responsible for all paperwork.

◆ You are responsible for liability and business debts.

◆ You don't share other people's expertise, fresh ideas and experience thereby, perhaps, limiting your business.

◆ It can be lonely running your own business.

Partnerships

You may be working as an active partner, one who is involved on a daily basis; a dormant partner who is a financial backer; or a silent one offering a name which lends some weight in the business. Rick Stein, for example, is a silent partner in *Sam's Brasserie*, London.

If you are entering the business with a partner or partners, there is a strong case for setting up a partnership agreement in conjunction with a lawyer.

Some points to consider:

◆ The name, location and purpose of the partnership.

◆ What each partner brings financially to the business.

◆ What strengths each partner contributes to the business.

◆ What equipment/finance each partner contributes to the business.

◆ How business expenses will be handled.

◆ What each partner is responsible for in detail.

◆ What each partner will receive for a salary.

◆ How the profits and losses are to be distributed to partners.

◆ How accounts are to be handled.

◆ How the partnership can be modified or terminated.

In a partnership, all partners are jointly liable for debts. If you come up against a legal problem you will be risking your personal assets.

> Sam's Brasserie's partners include Rick Stein, a silent partner, and restaurateur Rebecca Mascarenhas who offers advice on licensing, personnel and number-crunching issues. Choose partners who can bring different strengths to the table.

Forming a limited company

The same principles apply to forming a company as a partnership (see above). The company is the business and directors are the shareholders. A limited company means that the company, not the individual directors, is liable for any debts.

If forming a company, do shop around for a solicitor's package deal. If you decide to operate as a company you will have to pay corporation tax and make company tax returns. Soon after the end of the accounting period the Inland Revenue will send you a notice asking you to make a company tax return.

> Your local Enterprise Agency (www.enterprise-centre.co.uk or info@ enterprise-centre.co.uk) can explain the advantages and disadvantages of being a sole trade or forming a company.

Company tax

Before setting up a company, consult an accountant regarding corporation tax. Unlike a sole trade or partnership, company tax needs to be audited (though, depending on turnover, this can be very limited in its scope), which is an added expense.

◆ You must normally pay any tax due by nine months and one day after the end of the accounting period. If you have not completed your company tax return at that point you must make an estimate of what you think is due and pay that.

◆ Send a completed tax return, including your accounts and tax computations to the Inland Revenue by the filing date which is usually twelve months after the end of the accounting period. If the return is not delivered by this date, a penalty will occur.

◆ Speak to your accountant or tax advisor to decide on the accounting period and tell your tax office. Work out the dates by which you need to pay tax and make your company tax return.

◆ Plan ahead to make sure that accounts and tax computations are prepared in good time for this, but always communicate with your tax office if you fall behind. Make sure it's a two way dialogue for peace of mind.

◆ Keep proper business records and keep these for six years after the end of the accounting period.

Buying an existing business

It may seem like an easy option to buy an existing business, which is ready-made with staff, customers, premises, equipment and a good reputation. First, decide if you:

◆ have enough funding to buy the premises and run it for several months until you get established. Think about how much you will need;

◆ have sufficient business, finance and restaurant experience to take over the business;

◆ are physically and mentally able to work a very long day: 14–16 hours on average.

Top tips for buying a business

◆ Make absolutely sure that the business you are buying has good records and book-keeping. You must know the annual turnover and profit for at least three years to be able to determine if the business is viable and that you are making a sound purchase.

◆ Always use a solicitor and an accountant. The accountant will be able to help you determine a fair price. He or she will be aware of sharp practices and if the book-keeping has been done professionally or not.

◆ Be aware that the seller may augment figures to make the gross annual profit and net profits look very high. Obviously, if these are both high then the business looks very successful and therefore a good bet. But is it?

◆ Discuss the staff with the seller. How many staff are employed/semi-employed? What is the rate of pay, travel expenses, the package offered to staff (e.g. pension, sickness benefit)?

◆ Look at the profit margins. Are there any outstanding debts with suppliers?

◆ Don't accept the asking price of the business. It is time to bargain. You should take into consideration the state of the kitchens and all areas, the age of any equipment and the turnover. Use your lawyer for the actual negotiations, but make sure you are involved at all levels of the transactions.

And before signing the agreement:

◆ ask the seller for a thorough inventory of the kitchen and any hire equipment such as refrigeration, office furniture and all cutlery, glass, tableware and furniture, right down to the bins;

◆ make sure you have all relevant details of customers who may exist so that you can contact them via a newsletter informing them of the change of ownership, of your future plans and with any promotions.

Becoming a partner in an existing business

If you have worked in the hospitality business and have gained excellent experience and skills along the way, you may wish to move up the business ladder and work alongside a partner in an existing business.

It goes without saying that any agreement you enter into with a partner must be documented in full and be legally binding. You will need to find a lawyer who deals in partnership law. They will advise you on what you need to do and what costs are involved in setting up a partnership.

There are different kinds of partnerships. You may wish to join a friend, colleague, acquaintance or complete stranger who has the business and is looking for expansion.

Before you commit to partnership, think through the following:

◆ You should have the same aims and aspirations as your partner.

◆ You should have the same standards, attention to detail and work ethic.

◆ If there might be clashes regarding issues such as menus or treatment of customers and staff, discuss them at length to come to an agreed conclusion.

◆ Look at the different strengths you and your partner(s) can offer the business so that it is a stronger company. Perhaps you have a good grasp of accountancy, and your prospective partner is strong in marketing.

◆ All partners should take on equal responsibilities if you are equal partners. Make sure you spell out these and the percentage of the profits for each partner.

◆ If you are a junior partner (one who has less experience and doesn't have the same amount of money) with less than half the ownership, have each partners' work description written up, or you may end up with more of the dogsbody, menial work.

◆ Make sure that you have a list of all the contributions each person makes to the partnership. For example, who put up the cash, who owns the property, what equipment belongs to which partner. Draw up an agreement with a solicitor.

The advantages of a partnership are manifold and include the possibility of taking a holiday without closing the business, if you don't have appropriate managerial staff, and sharing the strengths of each partner.

The agreement should contain provisions for buying the other partner out, should this arise, and what happens if one partner dies.

Further finance advice and compiling a business plan are in Chapter 6.

4

Your property

You may have narrowed down the area where you wish to run your business but you must then decide whether to buy or rent a property. First you will need to contact commercial property estate agents if you are buying a pub to set up as a gastropub or a restaurant to create your brasserie. Or you may be looking at taking over a pub either as a tenant on a leasehold or freehold basis. You could also be thinking of leasing a property for your brasserie.

This chapter deals with how to negotiate the property ladder you are about to undertake in this, your most important decision of setting up your business.

It covers:

◆ location;

◆ how to locate properties;

◆ pub tenancies and agreements;

◆ freehold tenancies;

◆ general property leases;

◆ freehold properties;

◆ how to assess the potential business profitability;

◆ first steps on the property ladder;

◆ the property and timing – from viewing to signing a contract.

It will also deal with:

◆ local government and your business;

◆ layout of the kitchen;

◆ ventilation requirements;

◆ hygiene facilities;

◆ water supply and drainage;

◆ refuse collection;

◆ pest control;

◆ first impressions of your business to customers.

Location, location, location

The popular conception for a truly successful restaurant is that the three L's are sacrosant and it's no different for gastropubs and brasseries.

In a city, customers are close by, whether they live, work or are staying in hotels near to your business. By contrast, some of the most successful restaurants are in remote areas, so how do they create a good, solid customer base? Thanks to the superb ingredients cooked to a high standard and the sheer beauty of the location, people will make the detour to a well-run, perhaps seasonal, restaurant.

You've decided on your area and are thinking of buying or renting a property. Visit it a number of times on different days and and at different times of day. This will give you a better flavour of the area, the type of people, the activity, and it will also give you a more informed view of the property. Does the lighting need improving, the decoration, the entrance made more welcoming and accessible?

If possible, sit for a time in the restaurants you have narrowed down and imagine your own business working in the setting. Does it suit your plans? Is it enhanced by a view, a character? Are the proportions right?

Outline your plans to friends and talk over the space with them. They may be able to throw light on a particular problem that has so far eluded you. Or they may give good advice as to why not to open such a place in the area.

Put yourself in your customers' shoes. If competitors are based in the same area, are there too many of the same type of gastropubs or brasseries as yours? You may struggle for business unless you offer something quite different. But, equally, you may pick up overflow from successful nearby restaurants, the public seeing the area as an eating-out zone.

There is usually a good reason for a gastronomic desert. Look at Guildford in Surrey. There are very few good restaurants and nothing worth a mention in the *Good Food Guide*, for example. Why? Easy commuting into London where many commuting residents prefer eating out is one explanation. Expensive property is another. However, if a good gastropub opens in this area, it might be exactly what currently is missing – and in many other areas of Britain, too.

Where to look

For a brasserie, go straight to commercial property agents. Look in the *Yellow Pages*, *Caterer and Hotelkeeper* and other trade magazines to find them. Pubs are advertised in a variety of places too, including:

◆ brewery and pub company websites for tenancy and leasehold properties;

◆ pub valuer and business transfer agents websites for freehold and leasehold properties;

◆ *The Publican* and *Morning Advertiser*, licensed trade newspapers for freehold, leasehold and lease assignments;

◆ *Daltons Weekly* for freehold and leasehold properties;

◆ on the Internet search for 'pub for sale' or 'pub leases'.

◆ jot down pub for sale sign sellers' details;

◆ target breweries and pub companies in your area to find out what they may be able to offer.

Pub valuer and business transfer agents operate in the same way as estate agents with some companies specialising in the licensed trade. Others offer a broad range of businesses for sale. Ask to be put on their mailing list for details of pubs.

Pub tenancies and leases

An average tenancy or new lease will require capital in the region of £15,000 to £40,000 whereas an existing lease will cost around £75,000 to £150,000.

A tenancy is between the owner(s) of the property, usually a brewery or a pub company, and the tenant. The tenant runs the business as his or her own and pays all the bills. The tenant pays for the fixtures and fittings, gives a deposit to the owners and will pay a rent. Tenants may be 'tied' to buying certain drinks from the company. The bonus for being a tenant is being able to acquire a business for a relatively small amount, all agreements being protected by the Landlord & Tenant Act 1954.

Leased pubs are similar to a tenancy, agreements typically running between ten and 20 years. The differences are:

◆ A longer period of agreement for a lease.

◆ The ability to sell on the lease and to charge goodwill.

◆ The lessee is responsible for all repairs and decoration.

◆ The lessee will need a solicitor and property surveyor to set up the lease.

◆ The lessee is responsible for finding a buyer and negotiating a price for selling on the lease if sold before it expires.

◆ Running costs are higher due to additional repair, insurance and decoration expenses.

◆ Ongoing costs are higher due to legal and professional fees and stamp duty charges.

Freehold

Freehold means the property is yours if buying it outright, the average freehold pub costs from £300,000 to £500,000. Advantages:

◆ You can make your own decisions on how to run the business.

◆ You don't have to abide by brewery or pub company rules.

◆ You can plan long-term with no rent reviews or agreement renegotiations.

Obviously, when buying a property outright, whether it be a pub or a brasserie, all of the above applies.

General property leases

The average leasehold lease is 25 years, with other leases at 20 or 15 years but these can be negotiated with the landlord. A freehold lease's charges change only with the cost of borrowing.

◆ Landlords are looking for long-term investments and if the tenant has no track record, the landlord may ask for a rent deposit of a year in advance or a bank guarantee.

◆ However, the tenant may ask for a rent free period if money is being spent on the property such as re-wiring, re-decorating, new plumbing.

◆ The lease is a full repairing and insuring one with five year rent reviews, the rent only increasing, never decreasing.

◆ The amount of rent increase can be calculated on profits or a comparable method of calculation.

◆ A break clause is advisable. This is a walk-away sum should the lease be broken.

◆ A sub-let clause should also be included.

◆ It is, of course, advisable to get professional advice with a lease.

◆ The shorter the lease, the less security there is for the restaurant and its borrowing power.

◆ A longer lease could be used as security against a loan as well as a providing a feeling of security.

◆ Ask a tax advisor about setting off a large rent deposit against taxes as the period of non-profit making needs to be taken into account.

◆ Get the rent right as this is key to a successful restaurant.

Buying: leasehold or freehold properties

◆ Find an architect who deals in restaurant development to visit the property with you to discuss any alterations you may like to make: be guided by his or her expertise.

◆ Check on planning permission with the your local council regarding change of use, signage, access to property via new doors, and so on.

◆ Instruct a solicitor to act for you.

◆ Communication is vital between buyer and seller. Keep people up to speed.

◆ Discuss with environmental health officers basic requirements such as hand basins for staff, refrigeration, kitchen extractors, fire extinguishers (see below for a fuller view of the EHO's role and expectations) and so on.

Tips for buying or renting an established gastropub or brasserie

◆ Is the area saturated with similar businesses?

◆ Are the owners/lessees experiencing burnout, or are there other reasons for the sale/change of lease?

◆ Is there development in the area which will adversely affect the business? Or, conversely, add to the business's potential?

◆ How old is the business and how many years has it been profitable?

◆ What is the profit margin for the past few years?

◆ What percentage of repeat business is there?

◆ Do the books look accurate? Do the assets outweigh the liabilities?

◆ Ask your solicitor's or bank manager's advice.

◆ Have all renovations been undertaken with the necessary approval?

Shortlisting your properties

Be ruthless and only shortlist properties that fit the bill, otherwise you will be wasting time visiting unsuitable properties. When visiting any businesses, respect the current owner's/lessee's business so that conversations aren't overheard by customers or staff, as this could have an adverse effect on current business.

Viewing properties

Visit them at different times to see:

◆ what kind of customers they attract;

◆ existing facilities;

◆ the food and drink on offer;

◆ the general state of repair, standard of fixtures and fittings, delivery access;

◆ car parking.

Other tips:

◆ Good agents will get to know you and what you're after and will thus avoid introducing you to masses of properties that don't suit your wishes. What kind of property are you seeking? Make sure you get this across when in discussion with an agent, but be prepared to be flexible when viewing properties as you may surprise yourself.

◆ A drive around will help you to familiarise yourself with the area, who lives and works there and what the competition is like.

◆ Check out how prominent or hidden-away the property is.

◆ Check out the neighbourhood on-line for information on age profiles, employment, crime, housing and education, all of which is useful for your business plan.

> *For researching properties and their surrounding areas on the Internet you will need the property's postcode.*
> *See www.neighbourhood.statistics.gov.uk/dissemination and www.upmystreet.com for local information.*

How to assess the potential business's profitability

First of all you will need to find out from existing owners what running expenses they have so that you can work on your own profit forecast.

◆ If it is a pub, find out, for example, what products the pub has bought from the brewery or pub company.

◆ Overheads.

◆ Business rates.

◆ Energy costs.

Once you have this information you can look at potential revenues and then start to make profit forecasts.

First steps to take on the property ladder

◆ Get a solicitor who specialises in commercial property transactions for either renting or buying.

◆ Have a business plan that has been approved by a bank.

◆ If renting, prepare a good presentation pack to win the landlord's approval, adding graphics, particularly if in London where it is expected, for projecting that 'wow' factor.

◆ Out of town presentation doesn't need to be as sophisticated.

◆ Do put into the presentation the anticipated covers and spend per head and whether you intend to turn tables (i.e. use the same table several times at one sitting).

◆ First and foremost, however, there must be an excellent understanding of your market. This comes before entering into any contract, despite the excitement of falling in love with a property. Do you fit into this area? Who will your customers be?

The property

◆ If renting premises, measure the property yourself as the area given by estate agents or landlords could be inaccurate: the rent should reflect the actual space.

◆ Negotiate a lower rent if taking out a long lease.

◆ If the property needs repairs or major re-decoration, ask for a rent-free period or discount until these are carried out.

◆ Always get an agreement in writing for all dealings with landlords or estate agents, especially for any major alterations you would like to make to the property.

◆ Check on planning permission with your local council if putting up new signage or if you are intending to change the use of a property.

For a list of breweries and pub companies look at the British Beer and Pub Association website: www.beerandpub.com

From viewing to signing a contract

◆ The time taken from viewing to signing including legalities and licensing your property can vary from eight to 12 weeks depending on the complexities of the property and the availability of your finances. It can also be affected by your council's efficiency.

◆ If the restaurant is a shell and needs planning permission and licensing it may take three to five months.

◆ Change of use can take one month.

◆ Good communication is vital with all parties involved.

Local government and your business

You need to establish a relationship with your local authority for planning permission, building regulations and any structural changes you wish to make to the property. Are you converting or custom-building a property? It is vital to get their advice and/or permission before embarking on any building or rebuilding.

◆ Get approval for change of use permission if converting a property.

◆ Consider consulting a professional to sort out the paperwork if the process is complicated – and for your sanity.

◆ To lodge a complaint against your local authority if you feel the handling of your application was badly undertaken, contact the authority first then a higher authority if still dissatisfied. You may wish to discuss the possible steps with your solicitor or a professional planning consultant.

Scrutinising the exterior and interior of a property

View properties in great detail. This will help to negotiate your price as you discover things that need to be done. Have a list of work to discuss with builders for quotations, and check the following:

◆ Are there cracks or any visible structural problems?

◆ Are the ceilings flaking? Any damp patches?

◆ Is the flooring, particularly in the kitchen areas, suitable and in good condition?

◆ Is there good drainage?

◆ Does the flooring slope, have holes, have changes of level?

◆ Are kitchen surfaces and equipment surfaces in sound condition?

◆ Is there adequate lighting or does new lighting have to be installed?

◆ Do stairs have hand rails?

◆ Are windows in good order? Check for rotting wood.

◆ Is the roof sound?

◆ Does the whole property need to be redecorated?

◆ Is there good ventilation?

◆ Is there an adequate supply of hot water and drinking water?

◆ Is appropriate fire safety installed?

◆ If equipment such as fridges and cookers are included in the deal, are they moveable to clean behind, in good working order, well maintained and clean?

Kitchen layout

To provide a safe working environment and to avoid cross contamination of food at all stages the design of your kitchen and service areas is of great importance. Your layout should be built around the operation and not the other way around. Points to consider include:

◆ The same basic rules apply irrespective of size or scale of the establishment.

◆ An older building such as a 17th-century cottage-cum-restaurant may not have the perfect layout. Take this into consideration when looking at properties, and decide if the areas can be made to work – or not. Can staff in the working area carry out work safely?

◆ A logical flow of operation of delivery, storage, prepping, cooking, serving, disposal of waste, rubbish storage and collection, with as many clearly designated areas for each stage of work as possible, is necessary to avoid cross contamination. For example, a box is delivered and is put down on the counter where chicken is being prepared. Not only can the box have dirt on the bottom, but it may now have been contaminated by raw chicken. That box may be moved to another part of the kitchen and the cross contamination is now in its second stage. The kitchen counter may also be contaminated from dirt on the box, the

29

box perhaps having been put down on the pavement prior to been taken into the restaurant. All of this can be avoided if a logical flow – and common sense – is adhered to.

◆ Is space limited so that efficiency is impaired?

◆ Is cleaning difficult?

◆ Is there sufficient space for people to work at benches (counters to you and me) and other fixed equipment to allow others to pass?

◆ The layout of cookers, ovens, fryers, refrigeration and other hot machinery, with or without moving parts, must be taken into account to avoid congestion.

Ventilation requirements

Good ventilation provides a comfortable working environment, reduces humidity, removes contaminated greasy air, steam and cooking smells. It also prevents condensation which will ultimately help in terms of redecoration and maintenance.

High temperatures and humidity will increase the risk of food poisoning. Good maintenance is essential to remain effective. External ducts require planning permission in most cases, and also need to be positioned carefully to avoid falling-out with neighbours.

There are three main types of ventilation:

◆ **Natural ventilation**: only suitable for small scale operations, this system is seldom ideal as it relies on open windows and doors, is subject to changing weather and is least effective in hot weather. Mesh screening is necessary to keep out flying insects.

◆ **Extract only system**: a simple, inexpensive technique which uses an extractor fan to draw out hot or stale air, cooking fumes and steam. Useful to ensure that cooking smells are prevented from spreading to other rooms.

◆ **Combined extract/inlet system**: the most efficient system with the fullest control, it balances the flow of air in and out of the area. The design is based on a combination of ducting and fan exhausting the hot, damp and sometimes greasy air from the area, with controllable replacement fresh air.

Hygiene facilities

Adequate water supply, wash basins, sinks, washing up equipment and good draining are of paramount importance in setting up your business.

Water supply and drainage

◆ Drinkable (also known as potable) water must be used to ensure food is not contaminated.

◆ Only use drinkable water to make ice cubes and to wash salads and fruit.

◆ Water from a storage tank or private water supply is to be monitored on a regular basis.

◆ In new premises, drinking water installations should be disinfected. Your local authority or architect can advise.

◆ Drainage facilities must be designed and constructed to avoid the risk of contamination of foodstuffs.

◆ All sink, wash basin and dishwasher pipes should discharge directly into the drainage system through a trapped gully to prevent foul odours.

◆ As this is a complex area with floor channels, deep seal gullies and sewers to consider, do contact your local authority for further information.

Sinks and washing up equipment

Adequate facilities for food preparation, staff use, crockery, general cleaning and disinfecting of work tools and equipment all require a well-sited and easily-cleaned supply of hot and cold water.

◆ Lavatories must not be next to food handling space.

◆ Hand-washing facilities must be provided in prep areas, with hot and cold water and materials for cleaning hands.

◆ Sinks for washing food must be separate from hand-washing sinks.

◆ Separate hand wash basins are recommended to be placed in each work and food service area, including the bar and preferably also at the entrance to the kitchen.

◆ Stainless steel wash basins are strongly recommended, but glazed ceramic basins are acceptable. Domestic sinks are not acceptable.

◆ Wash basins with foot, knee, 'automatically operated' taps or mixer taps are deemed a good idea, but are not necessary.

◆ Position hand dryers carefully so that dirt and bacteria aren't blown around food areas. As hand dryers are slow and inefficient and sometimes put off frequent hand washing or encourage incomplete drying, disposable towels are your best bet.

◆ One or more commercial quality, stainless steel sinks are recommended for the main sinks with one or more deep sink for pot washing.

◆ In large catering premises, separate sinks are required for each of the following: vegetables, salads, meat and fish.

◆ A dishwashing machine with a fitted water softener (for certain hard water areas) is recommended for all but the smallest of food premises.

◆ A double sink with double stainless steel, (never wooden) drainer is also recommended and may be used instead of a dishwasher but why be hard on yourself? Commercial dishwashers take very little time in comparison to domestic dishwashers to operate and are designed with a simple interior and simple controls.

◆ The bar might have a glass washing machine and/or a sink with double drainer.

◆ A separate sink for mops, buckets, etc. should be located outside the food area.

These are recommendations only. Take advice from your Environmental Health Officer, particularly if you have small premises with little space.

Refuse storage

Even smart restaurants like Rick Stein's Seafood Restaurant in Padstow have difficulties with rubbish due to lack of space outside. If you have the space, do position free standing bins well away from the view of diners, as they can be very off-putting. Some restaurants don't follow this advice. If you want repeat business, place bins discretely.

◆ Don't allow food waste and other refuse to accumulate in food-preparation rooms.

◆ Waste must be in closed, sound, easy to clean containers.

◆ Free-standing or wall mounted, lidded holders for plastic rubbish bags should be provided, or a foot operated plastic lidded bin lined with a plastic bag.

◆ Remove full bags and clean containers and surrounding area frequently.

◆ Refuse storage and removal must be arranged and designed to be protected from pests (flying insects, cats, dogs, foxes, etc.) and mustn't contaminate premises, drinking water or equipment.

◆ Either site externally with a roofed shield if space allows, or in a non-food area with plenty of ventilation.

◆ Keep wheeliebins clean and clearly marked with the restaurant name.

◆ For larger businesses, bulk collection of refuse can be arranged.

◆ Contact your local authority for what is on offer, as the type of service offered varies as well as charges. Contact them, too, for disposal of white goods (fridges and freezers, for example).

Pest control

Keeping those infestations of rodents, insects or other food pests out is a priority:

◆ Any infestation will lead to contamination of food and food surfaces, damage of food stocks and the building.

◆ To combat this, the maintenance of high standards of cleanliness, good housekeeping, food storage and pest-proofing of the building should be undertaken.

◆ Both country and town sites have vermin problems with cockroaches, mice, pharaoh ants (tiny brown ants) and rats, all of which can be dealt with by local authority or private contractor exterminators.

◆ The cleaner your restaurant (and that includes behind fridges, etc. where vermin love to congregate) the fewer problems you'll encounter.

Gloss paint encourages condensation, artex ceilings are not acceptable because they are difficult to clean, and polystyrene or acoustic tiles are unlikely to be passed by inspectors. Ceiling tiles should be fire retardant.

First impressions of your business are vital

◆ Is it welcoming and well kept?

◆ Is it well lit?

◆ Is there any cracked paint?

◆ Are the windows clean, the entrance swept and door handles polished?

◆ Are the menu and times of opening visible?

◆ Is the entrance to the car park clearly signed?

◆ If you have a garden and paths, are they well maintained?

◆ If these are overlooked, customers will ignore you and go elsewhere. If the property looks dirty, they'll wonder what the kitchens and toilets are like and, likewise, go elsewhere.

All properties need the basics over and above the obvious (a dining area, kitchen, loos): office space for paperwork, good storage space – other than the kitchen – for supplies including wine, rubbish (where is it to be stored until collection?) and staff lockers or storage areas for personal belongings.

> *Keep your entrance clutter-free for easy access for able-bodied and disabled customers alike.*

5

Licensing laws and regulations

There have been quite radical changes in law in the past few years in the UK regarding any business that serves alcohol to customers. Naturally, all of these businesses must be licensed, England and Wales, Scotland and Northern Ireland each having their own licensing laws. Reform took place in 2003 in England and Wales with full effect coming into being in November 2005 with the new Licensing Act. Recent smoking legislation in public places throughout the UK is also outlined in this chapter.

In Scotland, a recent review of the current legislation, the Licensing (Scotland) Act 1976 by the Nicholson committee, suggested wide changes which bring Scottish licensing law broadly into line with that applying to England and Wales. Please check with your local authority.

The licensing regulations in Northern Ireland, the Licensing (Northern Ireland) Order 1996, are currently under review and the consultation paper, *Liquor Licensing – The Way Forward* is to be decided upon in the summer of 2007. Again, please check with your local authority for the latest information.

Although all of the necessary regulations covered in this chapter may at first appear daunting, you will receive help all along the way from local authorities, the police and other sources. Most will apply to you. This chapter includes:

◆ alcohol licences;
◆ personal and premises licences;
◆ children on licensed premises;
◆ temporary or occasional events licences;

◆ public entertainment licences.

Also of importance are:

◆ Fire Safety Law;

◆ Health and Safety Law;

◆ RIDDOR (acronym for Reporting of Injuries, Diseases and Dangerous
 Occurances Regulations 1995);

◆ Performing Right Society regulations;

◆ Phonographic Performance Limited regulations;

◆ smoking;

◆ Disability Discrimination Act 1995;

◆ Sex Discrimination Act and Race Relations Act;

◆ Sale of Goods Descriptions Act;

◆ Price Marking (Food and Drink on Premises) order 1979;

◆ Hotel Proprietors' Act.

Alcohol licences

Under the Licensing Bill 2003, significant changes were made by the government
including providing that councils, not the magistrates' court, now deal with licences.
The following is now essential:

◆ All premises undertaking licensable activities must have a permitted licence.

◆ A designated premises supervisor must be named on the premise licence.

◆ Anyone who authorises the sale of alcohol must hold a personal licence.

A premises licence will be required by pubs, restaurants, businesses offering hot food
between 11 pm and 5 am, hotels, guest houses and other places that sell alcohol.

A Designated Premises Supervisor (DPS) is the point of contact for the licensing
authorities, the police or fire services. He or she must hold a personal licence and will
be the person in daily control of the business, and is also responsible for the supply of
alcohol, but can give authority to staff for sales.

A personal licence will be needed by anyone who allows the sale of alcohol and once issued is valid for ten years. There are various duties on holders of personal licences and the licence can be forfeited if the holder is convicted of certain offences. If a member of staff commits an offence under the Licensing Act, the DPS may be held responsible.

A personal licence holder must be over 18, not have any relevant criminal convictions as spelt out in the Act, possess an approved licensing qualification and pay the required fee.

The four licensing objectives are:

◆ prevention of crime and disorder;
◆ prevention of public nuisance;
◆ public safety;
◆ prevention of harm to children.

Premises licence

A premises licence can be granted either for a one-off event or indefinitely, applicants having to submit a plan of their building, an operating schedule (a brief description of how the premises will be operated safely) and a fee, expected to be in the region of £500 maximum. Contact your local authority to find out the cost.

The law relating to children on licensed premises

The legal drinking age is 18 although 16 and 17-year-olds can drink beer, wine or cider at a table with a meal, providing an adult over 18 is present.

Offences include:

◆ allowing children in if they are not accompanied by an adult;
◆ allowing children in during the hours of midnight and 5 am;
◆ purchasing or attempting to purchase alcohol for consumption by a child;
◆ buying or attempting to buy alcohol by a child.

These offences include infringements outside the main business premises, including beer gardens, terraces and any other outdoor areas.

The government supports the PASS (Proof of Age Standards Scheme) which approves and accredits proof of age schemes in the UK.

Temporary and occasional events

Licences are not needed for small events where fewer than 500 people are likely to attend. Licences are needed for the temporary sale or supply of alcohol for events where more than 500 attendees are expected.

A personal licence holder will be able to hold up to 50 temporary or occasional events a year at premises that are not licensed. Non-personal licence holders will be able to hold up to 5 temporary events a year.

A Temporary Event Notice must be given to the council at least ten days before an event of this sort, and the police may object to it on crime and disorder grounds. Contact your district council for guidance on how to obtain a licence and your local trading standards officer for alcohol measurement guidelines.

Public Entertainment Licences

If music, entertainment or dancing is to take place, a Public Entertainment Licence may be required. Contact your Environmental Health Officer who will also give advice on prevention of noise nuisance.

Health and safety law

Businesses have a duty to protect their customers and employees by making sure their premises are safe and without risks to health. The law includes the following:

◆ equipment is safe and safe work practices are followed;

◆ safe practices for the movement and storage of articles are followed;

◆ staff must be trained, informed and supervised about safety matters;

◆ adequate first-aid facilities must be provided;

◆ if employing more than five people, a health and safety policy statement must be drawn up and brought to the attention of all employees.

Accidents involving handling, lifting, tripping, carrying, being struck by a moving or falling object may occur on your premises. Look out for hazards, record your findings and act upon any potential dangers to either employees or customers. Visit the Health and Safety Executive website for further information on this important area of law: www.hse.gov.uk.

RIDDOR: notification of accidents

Employers must contact the Environmental Health Office of any fatality, major injury, accident, disease or dangerous occurrence that happens on their premises under the Reporting of Injuries, Diseases and Occurrences Regulations 1995. For further information see www.riddor.gov.uk.

Fire safety law

Revised fire safety laws – The Regulatory Reform (Fire Safety) Order 2005 – came into force in June 2005 and is applicable to England and Wales; Scotland and Northern Ireland have their own laws. The new law deals with:

◆ preventing fires and reducing risk;
◆ making it your responsibility to ensure the safety of everyone using your premises;
◆ doing away with the need for fire certificates.

Consult your local Fire Prevention Officer or the Department for Communities and Local Government: www.communities.gov.uk.

Recorded music

As a restaurant critic I receive letters on many aspects of restaurants from disgruntled customers, and music is high up on their list of pet hates. Often the music is played, seemingly, for the benefit of the staff: very loud and inappropriate music. When I suggest to restaurants that it might be turned down, I am often looked at with contempt. The message is that I am interrupting their party.

Music can, of course, enhance the atmosphere of a restaurant, putting people in the mood for a good time as soon as they enter the door. Conversely, it can alienate customers. If they need to shout to have a conversation, clearly this is unacceptable. More and more frequently this appears to be the case.

If your restaurant's atmosphere creates hushed tones, you may wish to inject some suitable music, but do listen to your customers. Often silence, that rare commodity, is golden and appreciated in our increasingly noisy society.

Performing Right Society

If you play recorded music in the restaurant you will need to have a licence from the Performing Right Society. The tariff applies to performances in the UK of copyright music within the Society's repertoire at hotels, restaurants, cafés, fast food outlets, banqueting suites, function rooms, boarding houses and guesthouses. Currently, only theatre restaurants, theatre cafés and similar premises are exempt.

The PRS, a non-profit making membership organisation of composers, songwriters, authors and publishers of music, collects and distributes music royalties. It also covers live music.

The amount you pay depends on:

◆ the type of equipment you use to play your music (radio, TV, DVD, etc.);

◆ the size of your venue;

◆ the frequency of the performances.

For further information contact the Performing Rights Society, email: musiclicence@prs.co.uk, www.prs.co.uk or call 0800 0684 828 for advice.

Phonographic Performance Limited

This organisation also collects performance royalties on behalf of over 3,000 record companies and 30,000 performers. It was set up in 1934 by the recording industry to grant licences for the playing or broadcasting of sound recordings such as CDs, tapes and records in public. If you do not take out a licence, you are infringing copyright. See www.ppluk.com.

Differences between the PRS and the PPL:

◆ The PRS distributes payments to composers and publishers.

◆ The PPL distributes payments to record companies and performers.

Smoking

From July 1 2007 it is illegal to smoke in any enclosed public space such as a pub, restaurant or office in England, with businesses facing fines of up to £2,500 if they break the law. Wales and Northern Ireland took the pledge in April 2007, Scotland in April 2006 with Ireland leading the way in 2004.

Other points in the legislation

◆ The ban includes tobacco or anything that contains tobacco or any other smoking substance including manufactured cigarettes, hand-rolled cigarettes, pipes and cigars.

◆ The legislation defines an enclosed space as one that has a ceiling or roof.

◆ Tents or marquees will also be classified as enclosed premises.

◆ Structures located outside premises may be designated as smoking areas as long as 50% of the structure isn't covered by walls or windows.

◆ There is no requirement to provide smoking shelters.

◆ Vehicles used by companies are to be smoke-free if more than one person is present.

◆ The local authority is responsible for enforcing the smoke-free regulations.

◆ All premises and vehicles must have no smoking signs. They must meet the requirements set out in the legislation.

◆ Failure to display no-smoking signs may result in a fixed penalty notice of £50 or a fine not exceeding £1,000.

For more information on UK smoking legislation consult the website of the Office of the Public Sector Information: www.opsi.gov.uk.

Staff smoking is a real problem, too, as smokers do often congregate outside the kitchen door in view of passing trade. This is unacceptable as it gives the wrong impression. Smoking, a real health hazard, also plays havoc with the taste buds as it dulls the palate. If your chefs smoke, what does this say about their tasting ability?

Disability Discrimination Act 1995

This act aims to protect disabled people in the following areas:

◆ employment;

◆ access to goods, facilities and services;

◆ management, buying and renting of land or property;

◆ education.

Consult your local planning department regarding disabled access, space within the restaurant and toilets designed for wheelchair access. An existing restaurant in an 18th-century building, for example, may not need to have a ramp, but any new builds have to conform to disability laws.

Amendments to The Disability Discrimination Act 1995 which took force in October 2004 requires that you may need to address any physical features which make it difficult to use your business. These include:

◆ steps, stairways, kerbs;

◆ parking, exterior surfaces and paving;

◆ building entrances and signage;

◆ toilet and washing facilities;

◆ public facilities;

◆ lifts and escalators.

In some cases cost or planning legislation may make it unreasonable to make these changes. Contact your local authority or consult the Disability Rights Commission website: www.drc.org.uk.

There are 8.5 million disabled people in the UK with one in four customers disabled or close to someone who is. The following is recommended:

◆ Think and plan ahead to meet the requirements of your disabled customer.

◆ Don't make assumptions about disabled people based on speculation and stereotypes.

◆ Communicate a positive policy to providing services to disabled customers and staff.

Sale of Goods and Trades Description

As a trader you must be aware of the Sale of Goods Act which implies that there is an unexpressed contract when you accept a customer's order, the customer may either demand a replacement for unacceptable 'goods'or may refuse to pay. Some examples:

◆ If the goods don't correspond with the description, e.g. roast chicken which has been poached or grilled instead.

◆ If artificial cream is offered, for example, instead of fresh cream.

◆ Even if the customer has partly or wholly consumed the food it makes no difference to their rights.

◆ If the food is inedible.

The Trades Description Act makes it a criminal offence to mis-describe goods or services. Watch out for the following:

◆ Wording on menus and wine lists.

◆ Describing food and drink to customers verbally.

◆ Describing services, e.g. cover and service charges or extras.

◆ Describing services on offer.

The defence – if someone is charged under the Act – is to prove that reasonable precautions were taken and that the problem was:

◆ the result of pure mistake;

◆ the result of information from someone else;

◆ the fault of someone else;

◆ the result of accident or other cause beyond the control of the person concerned;

◆ the result of the person charged not reasonably being able to know that the description was misleading.

Sex Discrimination Act and Race Relations Act

The Sex Discrimination Act and the Race Relations Act legislate against discrimination on grounds of colour, race, creed or sex. They cover the following:

◆ Refusing service to customers of particular colour, race, creed or sex.

◆ Refusing services by imposing unjustifiable conditions or requirements for these same groups of people.

◆ Victimisation through refusal of entry, providing services to minority customers which are inferior to those offered to the general public or which may only be available at a price premium.

The Hotel Proprietors' Act

This applies not only to hotels but those businesses which may have bedrooms on offer to customers; gastropubs are increasingly offering B&B. The premises' management is under no obligation to serve anyone unless customers are staying in a hotel or similar establishment. Reasons for refusal could be:

◆ there is no space left;

◆ the person is drunk;

◆ the person is under the influence of drugs;

◆ the customer is not suitably dressed;

◆ the person is a known trouble-maker;

◆ the person is an associate of a known trouble-maker;

◆ the person is under the legal minimum age for licensed premises or does not fit into the age policy set by the premises.

Under the Licensed Premises (Exclusion of Certain Persons) Act 1980 the licensee has the right to refuse entry to people who are drunk, violent and disorderly, quarrelsome or appear unable to pay.

Price Marking (Food and Drink on Premises) Order 1979

Prices of food and drink must be displayed in a clear and legible way by persons selling food for consumption on the premises. The following provisions must be taken into account:

◆ Menu and a drinks list must be at the entrance or be able to be read from the street. If the premises are part of a complex, the list must be shown at the entrance to the eating area.

◆ Both food and drink must be included.

◆ *Table d'hôte* (set menu) prices must be given.

◆ VAT must be included and a service and/or a cover charge must be shown as an amount or a percentage.

◆ Self-service premises must indicate prices where the customer chooses food and also at the entrance unless counter prices can be seen.

6

Business finances

When you are thinking about starting your business, it's easy to be put off by the daunting task of organising your finances. But, as any business person knows, this crucial part of your business must be dealt with meticulously, and on a regular, on-going basis.

If you don't have a head for figures, make sure that you have a partner who does or that you can rely on an accountant to deal with the necessary sums.

This chapter covers:

◆ your business plan;

◆ who should write your business plan;

◆ starting-up costs;

◆ your assets and liabilities;

◆ estimating your business finance;

◆ calculating menu costings;

◆ finding other sources of financing;

◆ raising capital;

◆ business partnerships;

◆ capital expenditure.

It also deals with

◆ next steps in finding finance;

- banking;
- credit and debit cards;
- book-keeping and accountancy;
- insurance;
- business rates;
- VAT;
- legal tips;
- useful contact websites.

I'll try to make this as engaging and informative as possible. Don't think you need to be word-perfect right away, but dip into the chapter to find the relevant information when needed.

A business plan

Having a business plan is not only important for your bank, it's also a great way to focus your ideas and work out if what you are planning really is viable. It is a written document that puts your ideas and objectives on paper which covers the property, management, marketing, finances, type of food and wine, staffing and all other aspects of your business.

Business plans are recommended by most experts, the banks in particular demanding them for further discussion.

Why do you need one?

- The process of putting one together means that you have done research and have considered all aspects of the business. This process makes you understand the business in more detail.
- A well-prepared business plan is essential for raising many types of finance and will give your would-be lenders confidence in you and your business.
- An impressive business plan given to breweries or pub companies will give you an edge over other applicants.
- The plan is a working tool – your map for success – and needs to be updated as your business progresses. It can be a great motivator.

These plans are, of course, not a guarantee of success but, by identifying the strengths and weaknesses of your ideas, you will greatly improve your chances of succeeding.

Contents

◆ The purpose of your business, your expertise and history and those of your partners, your staff (if you have a head chef lined up, for example), your Unique Selling Point (what is going to make it work and make a difference?).

◆ Executive summary: this describes the business in general terms. Make this short and to the point to make it easy for others to follow.

◆ Overview: your mission. What are you looking to achieve? Why do you think it will work? This should be clear and short too.

◆ Business environment: your market research into your type of restaurant; its potential in terms of location; problems and possible solutions; the competition; and expansion potential (running outside catering, for example).

◆ Finances: projected revenues, costs and profit.

◆ Make your presentation professional-looking. A messy jumble of ideas randomly put on paper will not improve anyone's chances of getting to the next stage of discussions. Instead, choose a business-like font, put ideas under headings, check the spelling and present it in a titled folder with, perhaps, some clear drawings. Make several copies to hand out.

Who should write your business plan?

◆ You, of course, to understand your business in all its aspects.

◆ You may like to enlist the help of an accountant or business advisors, an expert is seen as an advantage. If you don't understand finance forecasting, it may be wise to ask an accountant.

◆ It should, above all, contain what you feel comfortable in achieving, not the ideas of others on whom you may rely too much and which could lead to the detriment of your business.

Starting up costs

First of all, estimate your start-up costs. These checklists are a guideline.

Your capital costs include:

◆ your business premises;

◆ the equipment needed to start up your business;

◆ your marketing tools (e.g. printing of cards, menus, your telephone, mobile, website, computer and printing costs);

◆ initial office supplies (e.g. filing cabinet, book-keeping books);

◆ basic food and supplies (start-up basic ingredients such as dry goods – flour, pepper, salt, rice, pasta, olive oil);

◆ any legal costs;

◆ accountancy costs;

◆ loan charges.

Once you have made a list of these items, make another of estimated operating costs;

◆ utility costs (water, electricity, gas, phone, broadband);

◆ insurance cover;

◆ business rates;

◆ employee salaries;

◆ rent (if applicable);

◆ taxes;

◆ equipment maintenance (put aside a sum for this).

Estimating your business finance

A significant number of small businesses fail because they have under estimated their start-up capital, i.e. they start off without enough backing to pay monthly fixed expenses when the business isn't up to its fighting weight. Make sure you do your budgeting carefully and thoroughly before submitting your business plan.

It is important to estimate as accurately as possible. Forecasting exactly how many customers you will have is difficult to predict.

When you are estimating, think about the following:

◆ Are your projections credible and based on facts? Ask someone in the business or a friend in a profitable business to check your projected costs as you may have missed something out or under- or over-projected.

◆ Beware of carrying too much stock. Don't buy a wine bargain, for example, which may not meet with customer approval. Too many bags of rice or pasta may remain on the shelves and pass their sell-by dates.

◆ Estimate each costing including rent, rates, staff, travel and insurance.

◆ Don't forget quarterly expenses such as telephone, utilities, bank charges.

◆ Always review your finances and re-consider your options. Can you find a better rate for a loan, cheaper gas and telephone suppliers? Avoid financing that is too complex.

Your assets and liabilities

Before you go to the bank with your business plan, you need to think of your net financial worth. What are your assets and liabilities?

Assets

What do you have either short or long-term? A short-term asset is what you have in your bank account or something that can be turned into cash within a short period of time. If it can't be available for the foreseeable future (for several years, for example), then it's a long-term asset. Examples of these assets are stocks, bonds, saving certificates and premium bonds, car, house, furniture, jewellery and equipment.

Liabilities

A liability is something you are responsible for financially. For example:

◆ any outstanding loans;

◆ credit card payments;

◆ instalments on furniture, cars, appliances and other household items;

◆ outstanding taxes;

◆ mortgage.

Your assets should be greater than your liabilities. Go to your bank for advice on how to calculate this and then you will be clearer as to how to proceed in financing your venture.

Calculating menu costings

It is essential to cost your menus to build in a profit margin. In order to do this, you need to know the cost of each item that goes into a dish. This includes the butter or oil you may have used for the preparation of the dish, the garnish and the seasoning. Take into account tax and VAT.

Your gross profit – GP as it is known in the trade – is vital to get right.

The average GP for this sector is 60%, your costs being 40%. If you are running a more upmarket restaurant and sourcing quality produce, aim at 65% GP.

Some items will be cheaper than others to prepare. Do offset more expensive dishes by lowering the GP on these dishes and increasing the GP on the cheaper dishes. For example, a bacon and mushroom salad is cheaper and quicker to make than a salmon and prawn terrine. This is loss-leader practice and will help to increase the sales of the more expensive item but shoring up the cost by making a larger GP on cheaper dishes.

Before the net profit is calculated the cost of overheads is deducted from the gross profit including wages and running costs. Then deduct the loan repayments, interest and tax.

But, first, you will need to price items. Get price lists from wholesale companies, retail shops, farm shops, specialist mail order food companies and other sources.

At the beginning of your business, there could be a degree of wastage which will have an impact on your GP margins but this will be resolved in time once the business gets going with good management practices.

If buying an existing business, do approach the business figures with caution. They may not always be as buoyant as they appear. Study them in great detail and ask pertinent questions.

Gastropub/brasserie trading projections, a rough guide

Mon-Thurs	Covers	Av. spend	Multiply by	Total
Morning	20	£3	4	£240
Takeout Lunch	20	£4.50	4	£360
Lunch	15	£10	4	£600
Evening Meal	20	£25	4	£2,000
Drinks	20	£5.50	4	£440
Total				£3,640
Friday	Covers	Cost	Multiply by	Total
Morning	30	£3	1	£90
Takeout Lunch	20	£4.50	1	£90
Lunch	20	£10	1	£200
Evening Meal	40	£25	1	£1,000
Drinks	50	£7.50	1	£375
Total				£1,755
Saturday	Covers	Cost	Multiply by	Total
Morning	35	£4	1	£140
Takeout Lunch	10	£4.50	1	£45
Lunch	45	£10	1	£450
Evening Meal	45	£25	1	£1,125
Drinks	50	£10	1	£500
Total				£2,260
Sunday	Covers	Cost	Multiply by	Total
Breakfast/Brunch	20	£8.50	1	£170
Lunch	40	£15	1	£600
Drinks	30	£10	1	£300
Total				£1,070
				Total for the week £8,725
				Monthly average £37,808

Monthly Costs			
Rent/Rates	£2,500	Laundry	£300
Wages	£8,000	Breakages	£200
Food	£10,000	Promotion	£500
Wine	£600		
Utilities	£750		
Loan Servicing	£2,500		
		Total	£25,350

Monthly average less monthly costs £12,458 less VAT @ 17.5% £10,602

Raising capital

Aim to raise more money than you need. You often have only one chance of raising money – it is very difficult to ask the same source the second time around for more funding. If your figures are too low your business proposition may not work long-term.

Work out exactly how much you need and for how long. Re-mortgaging your house (should you have the luxury of owning one) would not be suitable if you need money for the short-term. If you need money to buy equipment, look at renting and leasing options.

Business partnership

If you are going into business alone or with a partner or forming a company with investors or lenders, think about the following:

◆ Choose your partners or investors with great care. Look for investors and/or partners who complement your strengths and weaknesses and vice versa. Clearly define areas of responsibility at the outset. These may shift as the business progresses, so discuss these changes in full when they arise.

◆ Keep the people who matter in the know. Your partners – should you have any – must be completely up-to-date with any transactions you may have made on behalf of the business. Communication is all when dealing with partners and those who fund your restaurant if you wish to stay in business.

◆ Aim for majority control with partners or investors as minor shareholders. But remember that you have to convince them that you are capable of running such a business.

◆ Outline and protect personal investment as well as the agreed split of assets and liabilities. Get it down on paper and get a lawyer. See Legal Tips later in this chapter.

Capital expenditure

The property:

◆ The property – its rent deposit, on-going rent or cost to buy.

◆ Renovations including labour and materials.

◆ Plumbing, electrical labour and materials.

◆ Décor including any artefacts.

◆ Toilet upgrade costs.

◆ Bar construction and refurbishing.

◆ Chairs, tables, service area costs.

◆ Floor covering, window blinds/curtains.

◆ Lighting.

◆ Heating, air conditioning, kitchen extractor fan.

◆ Fire extinguishers.

Kitchen and restaurant equipment

◆ Kitchen equipment large and small – from stoves to spoons. Include rental equipment costs.

◆ Glass, cutlery, crockery.

◆ Coffee/espresso machine – lease or buy.

◆ Cleaning costs including vacuum cleaners, window cleaners.

◆ Rubbish removal costs.

◆ Linen, napkins, glass cloths, kitchen uniform, waiting staff uniform.

◆ Laundry costs.

◆ Music system, speakers, recorded music and performing rights costs.

◆ Cash register.

◆ Opening stocks: food, alcohol, cleaning materials.

◆ Opening party costs.

Ancillary costs

◆ Telephones.

◆ Gas and electricity costs.

◆ Office equipment.

◆ Printing costs for menus, cards, publicity handouts, bill heads.

◆ Advertising costs.

◆ Promotional costs.

◆ Graphic costs.

◆ Menu research costs including travel.

◆ Exterior lighting and menu boards.

Accountancy and other costs including legal fees

◆ Accountant's and bookkeeper's fees.

◆ Legal fees.

◆ Rates.

◆ Insurance.

◆ Permits: fire, health, business licence.

◆ Licence fees.

◆ Staff costs – waiting, kitchen, cleaning, office.

◆ Breakages.

◆ Operating capital.

◆ Contingency fund.

Next steps in finding finance

It's time to persuade others to fund your venture with your business plan and capital costs worked out. The lender will want to see that the business will survive, so they can recoup the loan and the agreed interest.

You will need to satisfy the lender that your business has the right people running it and that you have done good research into the projected customer base.

Attracting financing tips

To attract financing it can also pay to have the following:

◆ Sales goals.

◆ Customer profiles.

◆ Economic environment (is there an economic slump or boom?).

◆ Trends in the restaurant trade.

◆ Competition.

◆ Marketing strategy.

◆ Key person résumés – you and your partner's strengths and backgrounds.

◆ Your chef's background and expertise (if you have a chef on board).

◆ Cash flow projection.

◆ Revenue projections.

◆ Tax projections – VAT included.

◆ Financing requirements: amount needed, detailed budget, repayment options.

◆ Bank documents.

◆ Again, this vital paperwork needs to be well presented in relevant titled folders and handed out with confidence.

Tackling difficulties in raising finance

Even with a viable business proposition, it can be hard sometimes to persuade banks or other financial institutions to support your application. But do persist and if you are unsuccessful at first, try again. It may well help to revise your plan if necessary; take on board things that have come up in your discussions with the bank.

As well as banks, look at alternative sources of finance. Make sure you have applied for all the help that is available from government and other public sector organisations such as Business Link (www.businesslink.gov.uk), the National Federation of Enterprise Agencies (support for start-ups: www.nfea.com), The Enterprise Centre (www.enterprise-centre.co.uk) and other helpful organisations.

The Enterprise Centres, for example will help by talking about your ideas with you in confidence. This gives you the chance to bounce ideas off someone who knows what it means to start a business. You can also get one-to-one advice on running and financing your business, as well as technical, legal and practical help, and you can join a range of start-up workshops, seminars and one-to-one advisory services.

You can also get step-by-step support on how to:

◆ put your business in action;

◆ research your ideas;

◆ plan your business;

◆ understand and plan finances;

◆ raise capital;

◆ understand and plan your marketing and sales;

◆ get your message across by marketing.

Business Link's *No Nonsense Guide* is an invaluable tool with information on forming a business, sorting out your tax and national insurance, what VAT means to your business, trading regulations, employees' rights and government advice and support. You can order a copy on www.businesslink.org.uk.

Banking

Talking to banks

One of the most important relationships you will have in business is with your bank. When choosing your bank, do so with care, ascertaining first what service and support you need. If you already have a bank account and are happy with the services offered, speak to them first, but shop around for the best deal.

The competition between banks to do business with you can be extensive, so search for deals on offer. But negotiate too. Stipulate your needs and suggest a rate of interest when you can start paying back the loan. It never hurts to ask.

Opening a business account

When opening an account, you may be asked for some if not all of the following so check before making an appointment to save time:

◆ letters of agreement regarding your property whether it is leased or bought;

◆ copies of property agreements;

◆ certificate of corporation if you have a limited company;

◆ a copy of a partnership agreement (if applicable);

◆ your driving licence or passport;

◆ utility bills.

It is advisable to open two types of accounts, one for day-to-day transactions and the other, an easy-access savings account for putting money aside for VAT payments and the like.

Bank charges

Bank charges vary from bank to bank, some typical chargeable transactions are:

◆ paying cash into your account;

◆ writing cheques;

◆ direct debit and standing orders;

◆ duplicate statements.

Bank charges add cost to your business, so compare different banks to find one to suit you. See www.moneyfactsonline.co.uk. Banking on-line helps to keep your charges down.

> *You don't have to bank with the bank that gives you a loan. If the loan comes from a non high street bank or is too far away from your business to pay money into, for example, bank elsewhere.*

On-line banking

On-line banking is a great boon to the busy restaurateur who can check accounts at any time of the day or night, set up direct debits, standing orders and make other transactions. You may also find that transaction charges are lower than those of high street banks or that they are free.

Business credit cards

A business credit card is invaluable for making purchases, some banks however require you to bank with them for a period of time before issuing you with one.

Accepting credit and debit card payments

In today's market, paying by card is the preferred method of payment. More than half of all adults regularly made debit or credit card purchases.

There are lots of benefits when customers pay by credit/debit card including:

◆ more customers through your door if they see their card is accepted;

◆ no cash restrictions can mean that customers spend more;

◆ increased turnover and profit;

◆ your banking becomes automated, making procedures simpler and faster.

Contact Visa or other credit or debit card companies to find out how to set up card payments. Negotiate charges with the card companies and renegotiate those charges a year after trading as they may see a good, profitable company in the making and wish to partake in your success long-term.

Running your business accounts

◆ Don't go over your agreed overdraft limit without prior agreement.

◆ Keep your bank up-to-date with any changes in your business.

◆ If you are experiencing any difficulties, talk to them.

◆ Check your bank statements regularly.

◆ Be organised and keep your banking information in an orderly way.

◆ Renegotiate terms with your bank and review your arrangements at least biannually for the best deal.

◆ Keep a good eye on your cash flow and plan for any shortages.

Book-keeping and accountancy

It is essential to set up good book-keeping practices from the beginning of the business so that investors, accountants and the Inland Revenue can see at a glance the cash flow, expenses and the profit and loss margins.

Record all transactions on computer if possible (buy a computer accounts package) as this will give you immediate information on the operation: the sales; stock turnover, sales per waiting staff and per table (very useful for checking facts if needed) as well as food and drink cost percentages. If you prefer to hire a book-keeper/accountant, add the cost of employing one into your legal and professional costs.

Choose an accountant who has experience and a liking of the restaurant trade and do a cash flow forecast together.

Book-keeping and accountancy requirements

You will need:

◆ cash and bank records;

◆ weekly sales of all aspects of the business (food and alcohol sales for example);

◆ weekly payments (suppliers, wages, rent, etc.).

Record the weekly income and expenditure on print-outs or summary sheets so that management can see at a glance where the money is going out and coming in.

The accountant will also require information regarding VAT, tips, credit card and cash sales, wages, purchases, operating costs (rent, rates, utilities, telephone, laundry, for example), drawings for investors and owners and capital costs (equipment, repairs, improvements, etc.).

This analysis of breaking down the business into the sum of its parts can be of immense help to see where the business is going, its strengths and weaknesses and its seasonal swings.

It can also be helpful in combating fraud and theft. If you see higher than usual meat bills, for example, but know that you haven't sold that much, it needs to be investigated.

At the end of the financial year, two summaries need to be prepared: the trading profit and loss accounts showing the gross and net profit, and the balance sheet showing the company's financial position. The latter shows the assets owned and the debts owed. The difference between the two is the capital value of the business, representing the capital invested by the owner/investors and the retained profits.

VAT

Value Added Tax (VAT) is a tax charged on most business transactions made in the UK or the Isle of Man, the restaurateur and other business men and women perhaps seen as unpaid government tax collectors.

VAT is also charged on goods and some services imported from places outside the European Union and on goods and some services coming into the UK from the other EU countries.

All goods and services that are VAT rated are called 'taxable supplies'. You must charge VAT on your taxable supplies from the date you first need to be registered.

You must register for VAT if you are in business and your taxable supplies, not just your profit, go over a certain limit. The current VAT registration threshold is £64,000 (2007) but you can opt to register for VAT if your taxable supplies (the amount going through the business, not just the profit) are less than this if what you do counts as a business for VAT purposes.

The benefits for registration under the limit include increased credibility for your business, but once you are registered, you will have to account for ouput tax on all your taxable supplies which are not zero rated. But also, you can take credit for any input tax on those taxable supplies.

You will also have to provide regular VAT returns and keep proper records and accounts so that VAT officers can examine them if necessary.

> *There are currently three rates of VAT:*
> - *17.5% – standard-rated supplies on most goods and services;*
> - *5% – reduced-rate supplies on fuel and power used in the home and by charities;*
> - *0% – zero-rated supplies which are non-chargeable. Examples include most food, books, newspapers and children's clothing.*

For small businesses, there are a number of simplified arrangements to make VAT accounting easier:

◆ **Cash accounting**: if your taxable turnover is under £600,000 a year you can arrange to account to Customs for VAT on the basis of cash received and paid rather than the invoice date or time of supply.

◆ **Annual accounting**: if your turnover is under £1.35m a year you can join the annual accounting scheme and send in just one return a year, rather than the standard quarterly returns.

◆ **Bad Debt Relief**: if you supply goods or services to a customer, but you are not paid, you may be able to claim relief from VAT on the debts.

◆ **Flat Rate Scheme**: you may be eligible if your turnover is under £150,000. It helps save on administration due to not accounting internally for VAT on each individual input and output. Payment is over a set percentage of the total turnover (including standard rate VAT).

Top tips for simplifying VAT for small businesses

◆ Registering for VAT may have major implications on your pricing structure, so always include these in any costings.

◆ Apply to register in plenty of time so that you get the help available to you, your VAT registration number in time for including on cards, invoices, etc.

◆ Be clear about the impact of VAT on your growing business turnover.

◆ Good book-keeping is vital for overall business management. Check documents you receive. You must have a VAT invoice to claim back VAT. A statement is not a proper invoice.

◆ Always enter cash receipts in your books before using the cash to make purchases.

◆ Many businesses take advantage of the VAT they've collected, making it work for them before being paid to HM Revenue & Customs. Pay the VAT into a separate bank account to accumulate interest. Be sure to keep the VAT collections for payment only to HM Revenue & Customs and not for other purposes.

◆ If you find yourself unable to send your VAT return or cheque on time call your VAT office on 0845 010 9000 and tell them why. Consider making a part payment to reduce the surcharge payment.

◆ Always quote your VAT number on correspondence or delays/confusion will occur.

◆ If you are not sure, ask. It's in both your and HM Revenue & Customs's interests to get things right. If in doubt, shout!

Payroll

Records must be kept of all staff, whether full or part-time. Avoid the temptation to pay unrecorded cash for labour as penalties for income fraud are severe. Records must include the following:

◆ Name and address of employee.

◆ Their tax code number and national insurance number.

Remember that restaurateurs are responsible for all income earned, including tips. Tax inspectors can estimate tip earnings if no service charge is included.

Insurance

You must be insured, and it's not cheap, so take time to find the right deal. Do spend time and effort talking to the right insurers – i.e. those dealing with the restaurant business – and getting several quotes. Or get in touch with an insurance broker. Ask those in the restaurant business which insurance companies they recommend.

Your business needs insurance for building and contents. It also needs liability cover for any litigation (such as a lawsuit or a dispute brought against the business). Even if you are able to cover the costs of replacement or repair, or any loss that may occur such as a shelf giving way with a hundred plates tumbling to the floor, it would be irresponsible not to be insured against any problems regarding customers' or employees' legal actions.

Your biggest risk of breakage or theft may be from your customers and staff. There is also the possibility of someone falling and injuring themselves in your restaurant or of the building itself needing modifying for safety.

Your insurance policy must include cover against fire, storm, tempest (however ancient this terminology is), burglary, malicious damage, breakages and public liability.

Your building and contents insurance should reflect all contents and all buildings independent of one another. Insurance is based on replacing and repairing, not on the market value or saleable value, so do ask a builder or valuer to provide you with an estimate. Then add a percentage on to this figure for removal of debris, architect's fees (if applicable) and any other costs.

Additional cover which you may wish to consider is business interruption which replaces lost income in the event of a claim where your business is interrupted. This could be the result of physical damage to your property resulting in your being unable to function as a restaurant. Generally premiums are based on your yearly income.

Insurance companies should continue with payments on this sort of policy until normal business can be resumed and you have regained the income you would normally expect. Income projections are based on the previous year's figures for the equivalent period. Even when the work to repair or replace is complete, it should pay out on a descending scale until your business returns to normal. Do ask for cover which guarantees you payment on a weekly basis for cash flow purposes and not payment once the claim value is known, some months after the event.

An insurance policy is a legal, binding contract with terms and conditions, so it is up to you to make sure that all items you wish to insure are covered.

Insurance details to look out for

◆ **The duty of disclosure**. This means that you give the insurance company all the information they need, and it is vitally important when confirming and agreeing to the conditions of the policy. The insurer must know what you wish to cover as the type of policy required must be an accurate reflection on your business. Be clear and specific and ask for written confirmation in all areas of your cover.

◆ **Public liability**. This covers injury and property damage caused by your personal negligence and/or business negligence.

◆ **Product liability**. This relates to any products you provide, but specifically to food you serve, either bought-in or food cooked on the premises. Should a customer find a nail in a roll (yes, it happened to me), you are liable.

◆ **Manager liability**. This covers you for staff looking after customers in the absence of the owner. Customers, when in sueing mood, will not only sue you and your business but also the staff representing you at the time.

◆ **A workers' compensation policy** should be discussed with your insurer.

> *If you have a personal accident and sickness/income policy it is advisable to continue with this.*

Legal tips

Don't put your personal assets at risk

If you are starting a business with one or more people, you can choose partnership, limited liability partnership or limited company status. In a partnership all partners are jointly and separately liable for debts. If you come up against a legal problem you will be risking your personal assets.

Put it in writing

Do put all your business deals and agreements in writing. If you have a verbal agreement, get confirmation in writing. A verbal agreement is often difficult to put into practice if problems arise. A written record will also prevent people from trying to change their minds, or giving you a different story at a later stage.

It pays to get advice early on

Get legal advice early on as it will pay in the long run. Problems can arise in the long-term if this is neglected. Ask for an estimate of the cost if you seek a lawyer's advice. If forming a company do shop around for a solicitor's package deal.

Get someone to recommend a solicitor

Solicitors specialise in many areas of the law and there are many different types of law, so this can be a daunting step. A recommendation from another company is a good start. Do ask solicitors for testimonials and references and follow these up.

Keep up to date with changes in the law

Employment law is constantly changing, so do keep up to date. Every employer must provide a statement of employment clearly laying down certain details. It can be in your interests to include policies that are not needed by law to safeguard you.

Business Debtline

Of course, the hope is that good finance and accountancy practices have been adhered to from the beginning in putting your business together. But there may be worrying times when some good, practical advice from experts would help enormously: the psychological boost of just talking to someone who deals with financial problems can be quite energising.

Contact Business Debtline (0800 197 6026), a national telephone service that offers free, confidential and independent advice to small businesses on tackling cashflow problems by:

◆ preparing a budget for your business;

◆ prioritising all your debts;

◆ dealing with court proceedings;

◆ understanding bankruptcy;

◆ avoiding repossession of your home and business;

◆ dealing with tax matters;

◆ negotiating with creditors and bailiffs and dealing with most other debt and cashflow issues that you and your business may face.

The Federation of Small Businesses is the leading organisation for small businesses in the UK and campaigns on their behalf to improve the financial and economic environment in which they operate. Alongside this influential lobbying, FSB members also enjoy a unique protection and benefits package providing instant access to legal and professional advice and support. For further details visit their website: www.fsb.org.uk.

Alternatively, there are two other useful contacts as well as government agencies and organisations that can help you make the right business decisions.

The Small Business Service (SBS), an organisation which operates a number of schemes and initiatives that are designed to help small businesses in a variety of ways. They encourage businesses to be more innovative and to exploit new technologies, they can help get finance more readily and they can also provide ways for businesses to measure and improve efficiency. Their website is www.businesslink.gov.uk.

The SBS also oversees the work of the network of local Business Link offices that operate throughout England. Similar services for lowland Scotland are Business Gateway, Business Information Source in Highland Scotland, Business Connect in Wales and the Local Economic Development Unit for Northern Ireland.

The business links provide independent and impartial advice, information and a range of services to help small firms and those starting up new businesses. Call Business Link on 0845 600 9006.

The British Chamber of Commerce (BCC) is the national face of the UK's network of accredited Chambers of Commerce and campaigns to reduce burdens on business and create a more favourable business environment. For further help contact the BCC's website: www.britishchambers.org.uk.

Useful contacts

Accountants

www.icaew.co.uk (England and Wales)

www.icas.org.uk (Scotland)

www.icai.ie (Ireland)

www.aat.co.uk

Alcohol Concern

www.alcoholconcern.org.uk

Banks

www.bba.org.uk

Better Payment Practice Group

For advice on getting paid on time and guidance on late payment legislation.

www.payontime.co.uk

Book-keepers

www.bookkeepers.org.uk

British Insurance Brokers Association

www.biba.org.uk

Business rates

www.mybusinessrates.gov.uk

Companies House

www.companieshouse.gov.uk

Criminal records check

www.disclosurescotland.co.uk

Customer service

www.instituteofcustomerservice.com

Environmental health

www.cieh.org

Federation of Small Businesses

www.fsb.org.uk

Finance

www.moneysupermarket.com

www.fsa.gov.uk

Finance and Leasing Association

Find out more about business asset finance: www.fla.org.uk

Food safety

www.food.gov.uk

www.foodlink.org.uk

www.allergyuk.org

Food legislation

www.food.gov.uk

www.foodstandards.gov.uk

Health and Safety Executive

Information on health and safety rules for small businesses: www.hse.gov.uk

Inland Revenue helpline for the newly self-employed

To register as self-employed if you are going into business as a sole trader or partnership: www.inlandrevenue.gov.uk

Inland Revenue self-assessment orderline

Forms, leaflets, factsheets: 0845 9000 404

Jobcentre Plus

www.jobcentreplus.gov.uk

Licensing law

www.culture.gov.uk

National Business Angels Network

www.bestmatch.co.uk

National Federation of Enterprise Agencies

www.nfea.com

Staff

www.workingintheuk.gov.uk

www.employmentribunals.gov.uk

www.acas.org.uk

www.cipd.co.uk

Stamp duty

www.inlandrevenue.gov.uk

Trading Standards Institute

www.tradingstandards.gov.uk

Valuation Office Agency

Information on non-domestic rates payable on business premises

VAT and tax

www.hmrc.gov.uk

www.tax.org.uk

Waste

www.envirowise.gov.uk

7

Design and equipment for the kitchen and restaurant

This chapter deals with design. Careful design defines how functional the overall restaurant and kitchen can be. It will also help you with:

◆ the choice of chairs and tables;

◆ tips on flooring, walls and ceilings, toilets, lighting;

◆ how to dress a restaurant table.

Gastropubs and brasseries have two distinctive styles which are also different from that of the average restaurant: we'll look at these differences in this chapter.

The chapter also looks at kitchen design, plus kitchen equipment – from a lemon squeezer to a fridge and stove. We'll also consider china, glass, cutlery and that all-important service from kitchen to restaurant and back again.

Design

The designer Stephen Bayley says of the restaurant trade: 'Food and design are philosophically linked. Good food has to be nutritious, taste good and look appetising. Good design has to work well, be visually pleasing and easy to use.' In other words, keep it simple, don't over-complicate anything. Less is more!

The other holy grail, besides good food and design, is 'buzz'. This can be encouraged by design by making the space work and giving it energy.

Restaurants can also be described in a dispassionate way, the kitchen as the factory, the restaurant as the sales office and showroom. If you accept this more hard-headed approach, the better the planning and the outcome.

Restaurant design has changed considerably over the past decade or so. Professional designers mostly design with the 'wow' factor in mind, especially in corporate restaurant businesses. All that metal. All that 'leather' seating. All that minimalist lighting. And, to my mind, they all look the same.

The gastropub look

As mentioned in a previous chapter, the gastropub look is pretty uniform, despite the fact that many of their owners see their pubs as an extension of their uncomplicated, relaxed, *laissez-faire* attitude showing their individuality.

Possibly, the gastropub should have:

◆ stripped boards and tables;
◆ mismatched school furniture;
◆ banquettes;
◆ comfy sofas;
◆ polished wooden bar;
◆ 'nicotine'-stained walls;
◆ blackboard menus;
◆ open plan kitchen.

Of course, this look has been developed since London's *The Eagle* first opened its doors. Dark wood panelling, tablecloths, a dining room off the main bar, conservatory annexes and designer lounge areas can meet up with chic, architect-designed makeover without losing touch with its prime objective: the warmth of a pub serving good food. Some condemn this move from old-fashioned tarted-up boozer; there's no denying the attraction of this original gastropub.

The brasserie look

The much-loved typical brasserie look is one of nostalgia. However, modern brasseries emulate ordinary restaurants and could be indistinguishable from them. Bear in mind that the brasserie is essentially seen as a meeting place, a business that is open from early until late and must satisfy all the meals that these long opening hours entail, hence the style has to deal with such an influx of customers. Some, of course, are open only for set meal times. But are they the real thing?

London's *The Wolseley*, an all day café-brasserie in the grand European style, has got the look by the spade-full.

Nostalgic, the typical brasserie should have:

◆ mirrors;

◆ curtainless or café-curtained windows onto street;

◆ wood panelling;

◆ paintings and prints galore;

◆ marble or zinc-topped tables for coffee and patisserie or drinks;

◆ differing-sized tables, some with tablecloths for diners;

◆ long marble or wooden bar;

◆ banquettes;

◆ cream walls;

◆ newspapers on poles;

◆ immaculately dressed staff in long aprons;

◆ outdoor on-street tables under a canopy for drinks or light lunches.

This look has developed since the glory days of the Parisian brasserie with very sleek modernity taking over. Some of the new look may include blonde wood floors, spotlighting, differing table and chair heights, communal tables and benches, modern paintings, brightly painted walls, etched windows, more formal dining with tablecloths and wicker and metal outdoor seating.

Professional design

You must decide whether it necessary to go down the professional designer route to achieve either of these types of restaurants. The interior – and exterior – will convey to the public your taste, your style.

Do seek out some professional expertise before leaping into the unknown, or visit a variety of restaurants to pick up on some of the traits you wish to incorporate into your own. But beware of clashing styles, a cluttered look. An integrated, overall style has to emerge. Beware, too, of designs that do not focus on customers' and staff's basic needs – comfort and the ability to move around the area to serve at tables. The look has to be in proportion to the space.

If you count on the design only, leaving out the welcoming personality of the owner or manager, good, friendly service with a smile and quality food, the restaurant won't stand out from the crowd. You need all of these to create an appropriate environment.

Buy robust furniture which can withstand the hard wear and tear demanded in a public space. Visit specialist restaurant furniture shops and commercial kitchen businesses to see what is on offer.

But lack of design can also be effective; the gastropub, knowing its market, may go down the simplest of routes. Cobbling together pine tables and wooden chairs can achieve a popular look. It may also convey 'inexpensive meal out'. However, looks can be deceiving.

As a guide, an allowance of 2.5–4 square metres per person in the restaurant takes into consideration seating, table space, gangway and access to bar/counter.

Let's look at the layout and practicality of the premises.

A functional restaurant/pub

No matter how quirky or charming a restaurant is, it must be first and foremost functional. When looking at properties, look at the space from the point of view of being full. Imagine your restaurant with every table taken. Buzzing.

Now walk through the space from its entrance to the back of the restaurant and note the following:

◆ The shape: it may be too small or too large for your intended business. Or it may have awkwardly located doors, windows and access to the kitchen.

◆ The flow for customers and staff to reach tables, toilets, bar, kitchen.

◆ Signage. It may need changing or updating.

◆ The entrance: welcoming and well lit. Scrutinise where the coats can go, if the door handle is user-friendly. There may be a lot of steps.

◆ The area near the entrance should be draught-free. Customers will not return if their table is in the direct line of a blast of cold air. A double door lobby is one answer.

◆ The light switches need to be by the front and back door for easy access.

◆ A cloakroom area for coats, shopping bags and umbrellas is highly desirable, or your guests will clutter the restaurant with belongings.

◆ A good entry point for deliveries either at the front or back of the property.

◆ Décor: if funds are tight, it may cost too much to rectify.

Make a list of any improvements, decoration, signage, lighting, flooring and access that need to be made.

The entrance and bar

◆ Make your entrance welcoming and uncluttered for easy access into the restaurant and to be able to see and greet your customers.

◆ The bar is a focal point for both customers and staff. It stocks your drink, glasses, bottle fridges and other bar items including your coffee machine.

◆ The bar also acts as a control centre for ordering, making bills out, housing the cash register, taking bookings, making phone calls to suppliers and storing menus and wine lists.

◆ Place racks at the back of the bar for wine storage. Keep them stocked up as it adds to presentation as well as being practical.

◆ Keep the bar as spotless and as uncluttered as possible.

◆ If you have no space for a bar you will need to find space elsewhere for making out bills, opening wine, storing menus and all that goes with the smooth running of a restaurant.

The restaurant

Tables

The flow between customers, tables and staff is of paramount importance. If you put too many tables and chairs in an inappropriate space, it will cause discomfort to all. Your choice of table size and the type of chair is crucial. Points to look out for:

◆ Choices include round, square, rectangular tables for 2, 4, 6 and 8 diners, tables with legs or pedestals or with interchangeable round tops.

    ◆ 76cm square table seats two.

    ◆ 1m square seats four.

    ◆ 1m round seats four.

    ◆ 1.52m round seats eight.

    ◆ 137cm x 76cm rectangular table seats four.

◆ Zinc, marble, wood or other materials are possible surfaces. You may be thinking of a mix with tablecloths on some and not on others.

◆ Get accurate measurements of tables and chairs from a variety of manufacturers.

◆ Place markers or string around the restaurant before committing yourself to buying the furniture.

◆ Beware the furniture showroom look if there is too much furniture.

◆ If you have a designer, ask for a graphic design or a scale model to play with.

◆ Choose robust tables. They will last.

◆ With flexible seating, you will be able to plan for larger parties. You will need to know how many you can seat comfortably before taking a booking for a single, large party or several parties.

◆ Make sure you have reasonable staff access to each chair.

◆ Round tables can create problems with large parties as they can't be joined together. Buy tables with differing lift-off top sizes and shapes to add to your flexibility.

◆ Flow paths must be maintained from kitchen to tables and from bar to tables, as well as from and to the entrance and the toilets.

◆ Tables by the kitchen door are to be avoided at all costs. A swinging door nearby, staff flow and noise aren't acceptable. A table by the kitchen door is known in the trade as Siberia.

◆ Use this inhospitable space for a service station for napkins, cutlery, bread, condiments, candle holders and other items for use by staff to minimise their entry into the kitchen.

Chairs

Too many chair types are uncomfortable. Customers can be put off by the seating, so choose chairs that reflect your business. If customers are coming for a coffee or a drink, it isn't necessary to buy upholstered chairs. But, for more formal dining, the longer the stay, the better the chair needs to be. Points to consider:

◆ Beware of high backs, arm rests and bulky design if you have a small space. They will be taking up valuable space and might contribute to the furniture warehouse look.

◆ Chairs must be of a practical design if the whole restaurant is taken over for a party.

◆ Avoid making a costly mistake by choosing chairs for their aesthetic qualities. They may look smart, but are they up to the job?

◆ Your chairs must be able to stand up to extensive wear and tear.

◆ Bear in mind the increasing girth of the nation.

Other chair considerations

◆ Ask a manufacturer to come up with a design to suit your restaurant or choose chairs from a range of designs on the market.

◆ Take a few sample chairs home with you to sit on for a several days to find the most comfortable.

◆ A chair seat is usually 46 cm from the ground, its depth from the front edge of the seat to the back of the chair is also 46 cm. The height from the ground to the top of the back is 1 m.

◆ Choose chairs that can stack so that you can store them without taking up too much room if you need to store extra ones and space is tight.

◆ Customers rock backwards on their chairs, so choose a robust chair with splayed legs with a robust frame.

◆ For a more casual, quick-turnaround restaurant you still need a chair that is reasonably comfortable and not one that catches you in the backs of the thighs.

◆ Most modern chairs are wooden or constructed from a mixture of metal and wood and can make a lot of noise on a wooden floor. Ask the advice of the salesperson or manufacturer as to how this can be overcome. It can be very distracting for diners and staff.

◆ Banquettes are increasingly popular in both gastropubs and brasseries but they are inflexible. Benches at communal tables are also being seen more.

Flooring, walls and ceilings

◆ Wood flooring is **the** chosen flooring for new and re-vamped restaurants. It looks smart, clean and light and is easy to maintain.

◆ Drawbacks: high volume noise levels with chairs scraping the floor.

◆ There is no cushioning of noise with wood flooring – voices, plates, cutlery, music are soaked up by carpeting.

◆ Carpets stain, absorb smells, need more cleaning and don't have the longevity of wood flooring. It can also absorb noise and therefore lessen the character of a bustling, buzzing place.

◆ A mix of carpet and wood can add atmosphere and help noise levels.

◆ Absorbent materials for the ceiling will help to control noise. Too low a ceiling will add to heat and noise.

◆ Lighting and electrical points must be finalised before decoration.

◆ Consider installing under-floor heating before laying flooring.

◆ Put in ventilation (and air-conditioning, too, if this is your choice) before work on the ceiling.

Toilets

Toilets are often last on the list of important items. But this is a mistake as most customers recoil on being forced to use poorly maintained, old toilets and often will cross restaurants off their list that neglect this item.

However, increasingly a new breed of toilet is making its mark. Smart stand alone bowls, mixer taps (and not before time!), innovative glass panels, good-sized mirrors, ventilation and subdued flattering lighting are just some design features. It shows a respect for the customer, even if the customer doesn't reciprocate in quite the same way.

Some points:

◆ Make sure that the signage to toilets is clear.

◆ Designate staff to keep the toilets clean during opening hours to alleviate used paper towels, dirty sinks, toilet paper on cubicle floors and overflowing bins.

◆ Have a weekly rota of staff, too, to carry out checks before each service.

◆ Design the toilets for easy maintenance.

◆ If the toilets are small don't install a hand dryer which will heat up the room to uncomfortable levels. Put in paper towels instead or an extending towel roller. Hand dryers add to the noise level, their efficiency questionable.

◆ Make sure all toilet cubicle locks work and are maintained.

◆ If the toilets are close to tables, make sure there is a door to the area that is self-closing. And doesn't squeak.

◆ Do the toilets smell sweet? If not, why not?

◆ Supply liquid soaps that are securely attached to stop theft.

◆ Avoid 'funny' names such as Tou Louse (geddit?), Little Boys and Little Girls rooms, etc.

◆ Keep toilets simple yet smart. Add a bit of colour if your restaurant has muted shades.

Lighting

Good, well-designed lighting adds atmosphere, a warming colour and tone and makes the customers and food even more appealing. It can enhance the sense of theatre, all part of the restaurant buzz.

Some tips:

◆ Use dimmers to create instant atmosphere and mood, but don't make the restaurant too dark so that reading the menu, a wine list or paying the bill can become a trial.

◆ Light fixtures can be as decorative or unobtrusive as suits the décor.

◆ Avoid overhead lighting.

◆ Table lamps can work in some instances, but beware of looking like a lighting showroom with too many table lamps in a small area.

◆ Don't destroy the atmosphere by too bright a lighting in halls.

◆ Exterior lighting needs to be welcoming. Light up the mandatory menu frame by the door so that the menu can be easily read by passing trade.

Dressing a table

Table spacing is of great importance, especially in a more formal restaurant. However, gastropub and brasserie tables tend to be closer together than in a traditional restaurant, and this can add atmosphere. What you put on the table or leave off is vital. Some tips:

◆ Tablecloths and napkins are expensive to hire and launder.

◆ Factor the cost into the day-to-day restaurant expenses.

◆ Get several quotes from hire companies.

◆ If laundering linen in-house, make sure it is done properly.

◆ Cloths suit certain gastropubs and brasseries, not others.

◆ White or cream is best for showing off food, glasses and flowers and these colours add freshness and cleanliness.

◆ Dark cloths are gloomy and detract from the food and are usually made from synthetic material.

◆ Paper cloths, popular on the continent, are gaining in popularity here.

Napkins should be simply folded in half. Gone are the days of showing off your staff's origami skills. They have better things to do with their time and skills. Nor should napkins be picked up and draped over the customers' laps. This is unnecessary and usually an embarrassment to the customer.

If dressing your tables with flowers there is no need for an entire bouquet as a simple stemmed flower in clear glass vase will add class and colour. Tall flower arrangements should be avoided as customers may not be able to see one another.

Glasses

Your glassware will add to the appreciation of your wine, beer, water and other drinks. Here are some basic tips:

◆ Buy only clear, plain glasses.

◆ Buy stemmed wine glasses.

◆ Buy tapered wine glasses with a good bowl size.

◆ Buy leaded glassware for longevity.

◆ Avoid thick Paris goblets as they are obsolete.

◆ Avoid buying glasses for their looks alone.

◆ Avoid huge balloon glasses as cleaning and breakage issues arise.

◆ Always wash, then rinse in hot water to remove detergent which can kill wines.

◆ Polish with a clean cloth.

◆ Store upright, never on their rim.

◆ Buy the same design wine, water and juice glasses for consistency.

◆ To improve wine sales, use two sizes of wine glass (175ml, 250ml).

◆ Draught beer or cider must sold in half pints or multiples of half pints.

Cutlery

Cutlery deserves the same kind of scrutiny.

◆ When buying cutlery, try different patterns to check for comfort and practicality.

◆ Go for a simple, unfussy design which will not become dated.

◆ Go for quality as it won't tarnish.

◆ When setting up tables, just add the main course cutlery. Simple is best.

◆ Dessert spoons can double up as soup spoons.

◆ Fork and knife sizes can be the same size for first and main courses.

◆ Butter knives can double up as cheese knives.

◆ Choose your cutlery after your china. It has to complement the china and add to the style of the restaurant.

In today's eating out society sugar tongs, grapefruit spoons, asparagus holders, curved point cheese knives belong, thankfully, in the dainty past.

Look at plain patterns, either stainless steel or silver plate, that will last and not stain. Get a guarantee from the manufacturer regarding the life span, clean it well and store your cutlery with care to help to prolong its life.

Stainless steel is available in a variety of grades and is finished by different degrees of polishing: high polish, dull polish and a light matt.

Silver plate has two grades: standard for general use and a thicker grade for restaurant use.

Store your cutlery in individual drawers or spaces at a convenient height for staff. The use of long, rectangular baskets for a more casual restaurant is quite common. When drying cutlery, place on a tray to remove to storage space to reduce handling. Make sure that all cutlery, when placed on tables, is clean and untarnished.

Other table items

◆ Choose practical salt and pepper mills, but don't make them too covetable or they will walk.

◆ Choose user-friendly candles, not tall, precarious ones that can be knocked over or get in the way of service.

◆ If you must, put special deal, promotion or event cards on tables, but don't clutter the space with too many.

◆ Cotton or linen is best for tea and glass cloths.

◆ Tablecloth sizes:

  ◆ 137cm x 137cm to fit a table 76cm square or 1m round table;

  ◆ 183cm x 183cm to fit a table 1m square;

  ◆ 183cm x 244cm to fit rectangular table or;

  ◆ 183cm x 137cm to fit smaller rectangular table;

  ◆ slipcloths (to cover just the top of the tablecloth): 1m x 1m;

  ◆ linen napkins: 46–50cm square;

  ◆ buffet tablecloths: 2m x 4m – minimum size.

The kitchen

The hub of the restaurant has to work efficiently. Restaurants can fail as a result of a poorly designed kitchen, so it is important to consult a professional designer.

Another way is to ask a commercial kitchen equipment company for their advice. You may be taking over a premises that already has some equipment and adding other equipment to upgrade the kitchen. Or you may be starting from scratch. Do involve the chef, partners in the business, the builder, plumber, carpenter and architect in these crucial discussions, be it an upgrade or a whole new kitchen.

A restaurant kitchen is divided into four areas:

◆ prepping;
◆ cooking;
◆ washing up;
◆ service.

Storage takes place in all four areas.

A smaller kitchen operation may have to compromise on space, while larger kitchens will have the following prepping areas to function at speed:

◆ vegetables;
◆ fish;
◆ poultry;
◆ meat;
◆ desserts.

But the first consideration is what you expect the kitchen to achieve. Decide on:

◆ the kind of food on the menu;
◆ the kind of equipment you need and where it should be placed for efficiency and practicality;
◆ your budget.

Also take into consideration the following factors:

◆ future chefs being able to adapt to the current kitchen set up;

◆ basics like good knives, a solid cooker, large refrigerator and good storage space are prerequisites.

Kitchen and restaurant flow

The kitchen flow is important for deliveries to storage spaces and the flow of prepared food to tables and dirty dishes back to the kitchen. Some points to consider:

◆ Back door delivery access.
◆ Waiting staff may be responsible for the bread, the butter and other peripherals. A service station in the restaurant is best to access these rather than siting them in the kitchen.
◆ Extra clean cutlery and glasses to be located in the restaurant for laying up.
◆ If possible, have an in-door and an out-door to the kitchen to save staff colliding.

Your local environmental health officer should be consulted prior to work on the kitchen to ensure that all necessary steps are taken to abide by legislation. See Chapters 3 and 4 for the role of the EHO, information on ventilation, refuse, water, drainage, pest control, Food Safety Acts, disabled access and safety in the kitchen.

Kitchen equipment

Consult the *Yellow Pages* for catering companies that supply large equipment, pots and pans, clothing and knives. Ask friendly restaurateurs for their advice on where to shop and tips about their best buys.

Basic kitchen requirements

◆ A double oven with four or six gas burners and a solid top (a solid piece of metal that covers the whole stove, the burner underneath spreading heat all around for keeping items warm or for cooking when turned up).
◆ A grill or salamander (high level grill).
◆ A deep-fat fryer.
◆ A large commercial fridge or walk-in fridge.
◆ Under-counter refrigeration for ingredients during service.

◆ Freezer.

◆ Double sink.

◆ Hand basin.

◆ Washing up area with commercial dishwasher and storage shelving.

◆ Hot plate with infra red lamps if space and money allows (I found it invaluable in my restaurant kitchen) for plating up; situated where waiting staff can easily access it.

◆ A cool work surface for cold food and salad prep away from ovens.

◆ Work surfaces for prepping food and surfaces for food processors, for example.

◆ Hanging pot and pan rack to increase storage space near stoves.

◆ Good, accessible storage for cooking equipment, glasses, cutlery, serving dishes, plates.

◆ Time and motion studies to be worked out: plates near the plating area, coffee cups by the coffee prep area, for example.

◆ Rack for food orders.

◆ Good lighting and decent air flow.

◆ A telephone.

If using a microwave, make a space for it.

Other equipment to consider:

◆ Steamer.

◆ Griddle.

◆ Chargrill.

◆ Convection oven for pastry.

◆ Professional ice cream maker.

Other space requirements:

◆ Cool vegetable and fruit produce storage area away from heat.

◆ Dry goods storage away from heat.

◆ Non-food storage for linen.

◆ Non-food storage for cleaning materials, buckets, mops, light bulbs, toilet paper, refuse bags, vacuum cleaner, etc.

◆ Alcohol storage.

◆ Rubbish storage.

◆ Paperwork storage.

◆ Storage for staff belongings.

Buying equipment

Look for good, solid equipment on castors for easy cleaning and consider second-hand equipment for cutting down the cost of the kitchen. But buy sensibly, not just because it's a bargain.

The restaurant you are taking over may have suitable equipment included in the price. Make sure of the following:

◆ All equipment is in working order.

◆ Establish who services the equipment.

◆ Get any attached paperwork from the seller of the business.

◆ Insist that it is cleaned thoroughly before you take over the property.

> *If buying from specialists, ask for training to be given on the equipment to kitchen staff.*

Cookers

Gas or electricity? As any cook worth his or her salt will tell you, gas is far preferable as burners can be regulated so much more finely than electricity. A combination of gas burners and electric ovens is the choice of many chefs.

In convection ovens fans distribute the heat evenly, taking away the necessity of moving food around for uniform cooking. Baking temperatures are usually lower.

> *It is worth investing in a 'pass': usually a long, metal, lighted shelf for placing finished dishes prior to being checked before being delivered to tables.*

New equipment to look out for

New equipment is emerging all the time. Go to restaurant equipment shows, kitchen equipment showrooms, talk to restaurateurs and chefs or research the subject on the Internet. Look out for:

◆ Dishwashers with a good mix of low running costs, size and style.

◆ Double skinned dishwashers that help reduce heat loss.

◆ Induction planchas for cooking fish, vegetables and caramelising fruit.

◆ Pacojets which make sorbets, ice creams, pâtés, mousses and soups.

◆ Hold-O-Mats for keeping food hot or braising.

◆ Water baths for fish, terrines and vacuum-packed meat.

◆ Pass-through ovens, allowing chefs to work on both sides of the range.

◆ Ventless combination oven with microwave.

◆ Cutlery polishing machine which dries cutlery and removes water stains.

Always have a commercial dishwasher installed. It takes a fraction of the time of a domestic one, the interior is designed without frills to fit in the maximum dishes or pots and pans. There is usually a separate tray for glass washing.

Checklist of cooking equipment

◆ Heavy duty, cast iron frying pans.

◆ Sauté pans, shallow pans, dutch ovens (for braising, sautéing or stews).

◆ Pancake pan.

◆ Steamer.

◆ Cast iron casseroles with lids.

◆ Fish pan.

◆ Heavy based stock pots.

◆ Heavy based saucepans for sauces, etc.

◆ Knives for many uses – only buy good quality. They will last a lifetime – see next section.

◆ Chopping boards (see EHO guidelines).

◆ Plastic lidded containers for food storage and labels.

- Mixing bowls of all sizes.
- Measuring jugs.
- Kitchen scales.
- Whisks.
- Ladles.
- Large spoons.
- Slotted spoons.
- Kitchen scissors.
- Sieves and colanders.
- Chinois (fine sieve).
- Graters.
- Terrines, ramekin dishes.
- Roasting and baking trays.
- Pastry brushes.
- Spatulas.
- Lemon squeezer.
- Nutmeg grater.
- Fish slice.
- Pepper and salt mill.
- Apple corer.
- Funnel.
- Corkscrew.
- Lemon zester.
- Mandoline.
- Cheese grater.
- And anything else that is suited to your menu.

Basic knife list

Look out for Gustav, Emil & Ern, Sabatier, Sheffield Steel, Victorinox, Ed. Wustof, J. A. Henkels and Kin Knives, exceptional Japanese ones to suit all uses. It never pays to buy cheap knives. I still have most knives from my

1980s restaurant days which are in excellent condition. Chefs will provide their own sets which they have been built up over their career.

◆ Large chopping knife.

◆ Sharpening steel or electric/water sharpener.

◆ Palette knife.

◆ Carving knife.

◆ Chef's knife – 15cm.

◆ Medium knife – 20–25cm.

◆ Filleting knife (for fish).

◆ Several paring knives (like a vegetable knife).

◆ Potato peeler.

◆ Meat cleaver.

◆ Ham slicer with supple blade.

◆ Boning knife.

◆ Salmon knife.

◆ Bread knife.

◆ Cooking fork.

High carbon, stainless steel knives won't discolour or rust but will need more sharpening. The sharpest knives are made from carbon steel but can discolour when slicing onions or other acidic food.

If a carbon steel knife is badly discoloured, wet it, sprinkle with kitchen salt and rub vigorously with a cut lemon. A piece of burnt cork is useful for rusty knives.

◆ When buying knives look for balance and weight.

◆ Keep knives on a wall-mounted rack, never in a drawer with other equipment.

◆ Wash and dry knives immediately. Never soak them.

◆ Keep knives sharp at all times. Inexperienced staff using blunt knives can injure themselves.

◆ Look in the *Yellow Pages* for knife sharpeners who do the restaurant kitchen rounds or invest in an electric/water sharpener for in-house sharpening.

China or tableware

Depending on the style of the restaurant, choices are bone china which may be chosen by a no expenses-spared restaurant or earthenware, the most popular due to its strength and affordability. Stoneware, a natural, ceramic, durable finish is more costly than earthenware, but may suit a variety of gastropubs and brasseries.

To consider:

◆ As with tablecloths, white or cream tableware shows off food to best advantage and also blends in with all décor.

◆ There are many shapes, sizes and types of china to choose from for added style.

◆ Patterned china can become dated and tiresome if too busy a design, and it may also be difficult to replace long-term.

◆ Look for durability and rolled edges that can withstand lots of handling and washing.

◆ Make sure your chosen make is dishwasher-proof.

◆ Ask for a guarantee from the manufacturer that the chosen china will be around for many years to enable you to replace broken, chipped or 'gone-walking' items.

◆ If choosing super-sized plates, large soup bowls or rectangular shaped plates, think of the strength of your waiting staff's wrists and the extra miles they may have to walk if only two plates can be carried at one time.

◆ Angular designs may be more prone to chipping.

◆ Fewer super-sized crockery items will be able to fit into your dishwasher at one time, adding to your energy costs.

Amounts of china per restaurant cover

This is a rule of thumb amount. A gastropub will require less.

◆ 4 small plates.

◆ 4 medium sized plates.

◆ 2 large plates.

◆ 2 soup plates or bowls.

◆ 2 cups and saucers.

◆ 4 serving dishes (if plating main courses and serving vegetables or salads separately).

◆ 1½ butter dishes, milk jugs, sugar bowls, tea and coffee pots.

Before investing in china consider:

◆ The type of menu on offer.

◆ The maximum and average seating capacity.

◆ The rush hour turnover.

◆ The washing up facilities and capacity.

> *When storing and stacking china, don't go for the Great Wall of China but instead a mini one of no more than 24 plates to prevent a Great Fall!*

> *Contrary to popular belief, it is not necessary to have a huge kitchen to operate well. A galley kitchen can work excellently for a small restaurant as there is little walking involved and everything is to hand apart from, perhaps, the storage, fridges and freezer which will be nearby. A further, excellent advantage is that the kitchen is constantly being cleaned up as the chef(s) cook. A good rhythm is established by the chef.*

Service

As mentioned previously, it is important to get service right with flow from the kitchen to the restaurant and vice versa. When waiting staff come in with the order, or leave with the food, it is preferable that they do so with as little disturbance as possible, the collection point being as close to the door as can be achieved. Positioning of cleared items also needs to be thought out to achieve the smooth running of a restaurant kitchen and the restaurant.

Possible solutions:

◆ Arrange the orders in order of receipt on the check rack and remove when order has left.

◆ Plated food to be placed on the pass (see page 87) prior to being taken to the restaurant so it can keep warm.

◆ Position stacks of plates on a warmer or in a warming oven near the main ovens for plating up.

◆ Cold food to be removed from any refrigeration in good time for it to come close to, or reach, room temperature for optimum taste.

◆ Cheese should be brought to room temperature before service.

◆ Position washing up area and plate clearing strategically so that little overlap goes on and doesn't get in the way of the cooking area.

◆ It is important that these areas are hygienically separated.

8

Running a safe business

Running a safe, hygienic business is one of the biggest tests a restaurateur has to deal with. This chapter covers the restaurant's food hygiene, staff handling of the food and adhering to strict hygiene standards.

This chapter gives an outline of the Food Safety Act, the Food Premises Regulations, food hygiene training, temperature controls, foods that need chilling and those that don't. Food poisoning and the various types are also discussed in depth.

It also gives advice on staff hygiene and *When An Inspector Calls*: Environmental Health requirements and the visit by an inspector.

Legislation

Under new European legislation which took effect in January 2006, hygiene for all food businesses is laid down in EU Regulations 852/2004 and is embodied in the Food Hygiene Regulations 2005/2006 in England, Scotland, Wales and Northern Ireland.

Legislation includes:

◆ Selling (or keeping for sale) food that is unfit for people to eat.

◆ Causing food to be dangerous to health.

◆ Selling food that is not what the customer is entitled to expect, in terms of content or quality.

◆ Describing or presenting food in a way that is false or misleading.

The Food Standards Agency has a pack, *Safer Food, Better Business*, which you can download from their website (www.food.gov.uk/enforcement). It covers:

◆ Complying with the new regulations.

◆ Showing what you can do to make food safe.

◆ Training staff.

◆ Protecting your business reputation.

◆ Improving your business by wasting less, for example.

It is also available as hard copy: phone 0845 606 0667 (or email foodstandards@ ecgroup.co.uk). For Scotland, the pack is called *CookSafe* and *Safe Catering* in Northern Ireland. View all of these online at www.food.gov.uk and to view other information.

Registering your business

◆ You must register your business within 28 days before opening a new food business.

◆ Contact your local authority for the appropriate (and very straightforward) form. There is no charge.

Food hygiene training

◆ Regulations made under the Food Safety Act require that all persons who handle open food in the course of a food business receive food hygiene training.

◆ Short course levels are foundation, intermediate and advanced. Find out what courses are available from your local authority.

Legislative temperature controls covers:

◆ the temperature at which certain foods must be kept;

◆ which foods are exempt from specific temperature control;

◆ when the regulations allow flexibility.

In Scotland, Wales and Northern Ireland the regulations apply slightly differently from the rest of the UK, but the principles are the same. Contact your local authority.

Food safety management

Hazard Analysis and Critical Control Point (HACCP) is a structured approach which enables operators to put procedures in place to manage food safety.

To find out more about monitoring and taking remedial action, get the Food Standards Agency's *Safer Food, Better Business* or their *CookSafe*, both free guides.

Temperature control

◆ Refrigeration: 5°–8°C is effective to control bacteria multiplication.

◆ Freezing: –18°C prevents bacteria from multiplying.

◆ Cooking: 75°C is effective in destroying most types of bacteria.

◆ Hot holding: 63°C will control bacteria multiplication in hot food.

◆ Cooling: cool food as quickly as possible before refrigeration.

◆ Re-heating: 82°C is seen as a safe temperature.

Make sure you have a good temperature probe to test the core temperature of food. Buy a fridge thermometer and record a diary of temperatures for health and safety inspection. Keep it on the door to remind staff to check the temperature levels.

Foods that need chilling

Foods that need chilling include:

◆ Milk, yoghurt, cream, butter, foods with cream filling, dairy-based deserts and certain cheeses.

◆ Many cooked products until ready to eat cold or heated. Most foods containing eggs, meat, fish, dairy products, cereals, rice, pulses or vegetables and sandwich fillings containing these ingredients.

◆ Most smoked or cured products like hams unless the curing method means the product is not perishable at room temperature.

◆ Prepared ready-to-eat meals including prepared vegetables, salad leaves, coleslaw and products containing mayonnaise.

◆ Pizzas with meat, fish or vegetables.

◆ Foods with 'use by' and 'keep refrigerated' labels.

Foods that don't need chilling

These include:

◆ Some cured/smoked products.

◆ Bakery goods that don't contain cream.

◆ Canned and dried foods like pickles, jams, sauces.

These do need chilling once opened.

Mail-order food

Mail-order food must not be transported at temperatures that could cause a health risk. Therefore food that needs chilling should be delivered by chilled compartment vehicle or chilled packaging.

Food poisoning and avoiding contamination

As a restaurateur you and your staff need to understand what causes food poisoning and how it can be avoided. It is vital that your restaurant throughout is clean, and especially the kitchen. The food you serve must be absolutely safe and by following the hygiene and cross contamination rules, this will be achieved.

There are four micro-organisms that are the most common causes of food poisoning which, of course, make for alarming reading. But they are preventable:

◆ **Campylobacter**: the most common food poisoning bug in the UK. Found in raw and undercooked poultry, red meat, unpasteurised milk, untreated water. Just a piece of undercooked chicken can cause severe illness.

Symptoms: gastroenteritis with fever, abdominal cramps and diarrhoea that is often bloody. Can be fatal.

◆ **Salmonella**: the second most common food poisoning bug. Can be found in eggs, raw meat, poultry, unpasteurised milk, yeast and even pasta, coconut and chocolate. Grows very well in the food itself unless the food is chilled. It is also passed easily from person to person by poor hygiene such as not washing hands.

Symptoms: usually mild, with abdominal pain, diarrhoea and nausea, but rarely vomiting.

◆ **Clostridium perfringens**: the third most common bug and the least reported as symptoms are vague. Found in soil, sewage, animal manure and in the gut of animals and humans. Food cooked slowly in large quantities then left to stand for a long time is its breeding ground.

Symptoms: when taken in large numbers, the bacteria produce toxins which attack the gut lining causing diarrhoea and acute abdominal pain.

◆ **Listeria**: a food poisoning bug of particular danger to pregnant women, babies and the elderly. Found in soft, mould-ripened cheeses, pâtés, unpasteurised milk and shellfish. Resists heat, salt, nitrate and acidity better than many micro-organisms.

Symptoms: fever, headache, nausea and vomiting. Can be fatal to the elderly, immune-impaired infants and developing foetuses.

◆ **Scrombotoxin**: although not strictly speaking a bug, this poison is produced by certain bacteria in oily fish which has been allowed to spoil through inadequate refrigeration. It causes a dramatic histamine reaction. Found in fresh and tinned mackerel, tuna and – very rarely – Swiss cheese.

Symptoms: tingling or burning in the mouth, a rash on the face or upper body, itching, sweating and headache with a drop in blood pressure, abdominal pain, diarrhoea and vomiting.

◆ **E.coli 0157**: most strains of E.coli are harmless, but those producing the poison verocytoxin can cause severe illness, E.coli 0157 being one. Found in farm animals and land contaminated with their faeces. Transmitted through undercooked minced beef (such as burgers) and raw, inadequately pasteurised or contaminated milk.

Symptoms: abdominal cramps and bloody diarrhoea. In serious cases kidney failure, severe anaemia, neurological problems and death.

Measures to take to help avoid food poisoning

In order to combat food poisoning obtain good clear advice from your local authority health inspector. All food poisoning is possible to prevent if you are aware of it and how it can be avoided. Poisonings by salmonella and campylobacter are, however, on the increase due to a lack of understanding by those handling food. Common sense dictates that you avoid the following examples:

◆ leaving raw or cooked chicken out in a hot kitchen for several hours – and uncovered;

◆ preparing a sandwich on a board which has just been used for cutting up raw meat;

◆ keeping a bottle of milk on a hot window ledge for hours.

Heavy-duty plastic or polypropylene, colour-coded boards must also be used in a commercial kitchen and thoroughly scrubbed in hot, soapy water and rinsed after use to avoid cross-contamination and food poisoning. Also use an antibacterial spray with disposable kitchen towels.

A well-publicised case of food poisoning by a caterer at a wedding who left the entire buffet laid out in a hot marquee for over four hours, resulted in mass serious poisoning.

If refrigeration space is at a premium you may have to re-think your menu and your ordering.

Eggs

Eggs have been under scrutiny for many years, health and safety guidelines suggesting that raw or semi-cooked eggs may pose a salmonella food poisoning problem. All recipes printed in newspapers, magazines and books carry a warning not to serve undercooked eggs to the elderly or women who are pregnant.

So out of the window may go some of the most wonderful egg dishes such as Eggs Benedict, poached or lightly scrambled eggs and Hollandaise sauce. It is up to you to make this decision to serve eggs that aren't thoroughly cooked. Buy free-range or organic eggs to minimise any risk to health.

You may wish to add a note on the menu to inform customers saying that particular dishes contain lightly cooked or raw egg.

Staff hygiene

Staff must always wash their hands after using the toilet using soap and clean towels. Hand washing, too, must take place to avoid cross contamination after handling raw poultry, for example. Even if kitchen staff go out to the restaurant to check on a booking during work, they must wash their hands before resuming work.

Other points:

◆ Wash hands before starting work and after a break.

◆ Wash hands thoroughly after using the toilet or smoking.

◆ Wash hands after handling poultry, other raw foods and waste.

◆ Wash hands after cleaning.

◆ Hats to be worn by kitchen staff.

◆ Avoid fingers touching the face, nose, ears, hair or other parts of the body while working.

◆ Avoid sneezing or coughing over food or food surfaces.

◆ Hair to be tied back or covered.

◆ Cuts and sores to be covered with special blue coloured plasters.

◆ Avoid wearing jewellery as items can trap food.

◆ Wear suitable clothing.

◆ Change clothing regularly and launder clothing properly.

If staff illness occurs, legislation prohibits those suffering from working. Those having infected wounds, skin infections, sores, diarrhoea and carrying a disease such as hepatitis are barred from handling food or entering food premises to work. It is the restaurateur's responsibility to enforce this.

Cloths

Dishcloths and other cloths in the kitchen can be prime suspects in spreading germs. Use non-woven dishcloths rather than sponges as there are fewer traps for germs. Sponges also hold more water where bacteria can thrive.

Don't even think of using a cloth which is used on a counter to mop up the floor then used again for surface tops. Disinfect cloths in bleach regularly and dry flat, not scrunched up. Be a devil and throw them away after quite extensive use!

Change tea towels and hand towels often.

Environmental health requirements

The role of the Environmental Health Officer

Restaurant kitchens take a physical hammering with a lot of effort needed to promote the best standards of hygiene, cleanliness, stock care and food rotation. Take your eye off the ball – and your staff – and you could land up with hygiene and food safety issues. Witness Gordon Ramsay's television programme *Kitchen Nightmares* to note some poorly-run restaurant kitchens.

The policing of standards is the remit of your local council's Environmental Health Officers (EHOs) who enforce the law and, although the perception by some in the trade is one of draconian laws and over the top requirements, the system can't be bucked. Some of the requests are legally binding, others aren't. But their advice can be invaluable, particularly for those first starting up in the business or those whose standards have slipped.

> *EHOs can, by law, turn up unannounced at all reasonable hours and proceed to inspect your restaurant kitchen, toilets, storage space, the restaurant itself and your rubbish area. They may also visit as a result of a complaint.*

Some of the many items they will inspect are lids and labels on containers, the use of the right chopping boards, fridge and freezer temperatures. They will take a keen interest in the suitability and cleanliness of tiles, floor, walls and ceilings, storage, hand basins for staff, how raw and cooked meats are stored in the fridge, air circulation and vermin problems.

There are EHO horror stories: finding of stoves with no knobs on; staff turning the gas on with pliers; dirty, stale oil left in fryers and filthy fridges with no labelling on containers. They have also discovered babies' soiled nappies left in the kitchen; mould and mice droppings behind equipment; fire doors propped open with unsealed rubbish and cleaning fluids transferred to lemonade bottles.

What to do when your business is inspected

Some premises are inspected every six months, the majority far less often, mainly due to lack of manpower. An inspector, after showing identification, will carry out an inspection and then give feedback, for example, about identified hazards and guidance on how they can be avoided.

If there is a problem, you will be given the reasons in writing for any action you are asked to take. Where there is an apparent breach of law, it will be explained, and you will be given reasonable time to meet statutory requirements, except when there is an immediate risk to public health. You will also be informed of the procedures for appealing against local authority action.

Inspectors' powers

◆ They can take samples, photographs and inspect records.

◆ They may write informally to put right any problems they find.

◆ They may serve you with an improvement order where breaches of the law are identified which must be put right.

◆ They can detain or seize goods.

◆ In serious cases they may decide to recommend a prosecution.

◆ If there is an imminent health risk to consumers, inspectors can serve an emergency prohibition order which forbids the use of the premises or equipment which is backed up by the law courts.

Measures that can be taken if you disagree with the outcome

◆ Contact your local authority's head of environmental health or trading standards services to see if the matter can be resolved informally.

◆ If disagreement remains contact your local councillor.

◆ Contact your local authority or trade association if you think the law is being applied differently from other authorities. Ask about LACOTS (Local Authorities Co-ordinating Body on Food and Trading Standards).

◆ You have the right of appeal to a magistrates' court against an improvement notice or a refusal by a local authority to lift an emergency prohibition order made earlier by the court.

◆ A magistrates' court must confirm the emergency closure of a business or the seizure of food. If magistrates decide premises have been shut down without proper reason or food has been wrongly seized or detained, you have a right to compensation.

Other things that are taken into consideration are:

◆ The past history of the offence.

◆ The seriousness of the offence.

◆ The inspectors' confidence in the restaurant's management.

◆ The consequences of non compliance.

◆ The attitude of the operator/proprietor.

> *Your local authority is ready to help if you need any advice on food safety. Trade associations and independent consultancy services can also help.*

Safety in the kitchen

The following lists are basically common sense but, as a chef in charge of the kitchen or the proprietor, you are obliged to pass these basic safety precautions on to all staff taking part in food preparation and food service.

Hot food and liquids

◆ Don't leave metal implements such as spoons in boiling liquids.

◆ Don't overfill coffee pots, soup tureens, etc, with hot liquids.

◆ Get help when carrying large or heavy containers of hot food.

◆ Don't use a damp cloth to carry hot pans or oven dishes.

Cookers and electrical equipment

◆ Don't leave handles of cooking pans over gas flames or electric hobs or leave them over the front of cookers.

◆ Always remove the plug prior to cleaning electrical equipment.

◆ Always turn off gas and electrical appliances when not in use.

◆ Dangerous machinery such as meat slicers need to be adequately guarded.

◆ Avoid reaching over naked flames or hot hobs.

◆ Never pour water on a fat or oil fire, but smother it with a fire blanket or thick damp towel.

For gas safety, install a gas interlock system that cuts off gas flow in the event of kitchen ventilation fan failure. This is mandatory in most commercial kitchens. Ask your local authority for advice.

Knives

◆ When carrying knives hold the point downwards.

◆ Never attempt to catch a falling knife.

◆ Always use sharp knives. Blunt knives cause accidents due to applying too much pressure.

◆ Cut or chop on a board, not in the hand.

Spillages and other accidents

◆ Clean up any spillages immediately.

◆ Broken glass needs to wrapped up well before going into the bin.

◆ Avoid putting debris from ashtrays into bins containing paper as some of the cigarette ash may still be alight.

◆ Have a first aid box handy and topped up with sufficient coloured waterproof dressings and burns dressings. Be sure all staff know where it is situated.

Other equipment and storage

◆ Avoid the use of trays for multi-stacking of clean items like cutlery, glasses and plates. Use one for each for large loads.

◆ Never put cleaning or other fluids in bottles originally used for food or drink or use cups, glasses, soup bowls, etc. for storing cleaning agents.

Have a check list of procedures to carry out when food preparation has ended, for example: gas off, fridge door shut properly, back door locked, rubbish bags removed or tied to avoid pests.

Further information and useful contacts

You can get more information from the Food Standards Agency, the UK independent government agency providing advice and information to the public and government on food safety, diet and nutrition (www.food.gov.uk).

Some of their publications – all free – include:

◆ Food Safety Regulations.

◆ *Food Law Inspections and Your Business.*

◆ *Food Handlers: Fitness to Work.*

◆ *Eggs: What Caterers Need to Know.*

◆ *Dine Out, Eat Well.*

The Department of Trade and Industry (www.dti.gov.uk/publications or email publications@dti.gso.gov.uk) offer many publications including:

◆ Small Business Service.

◆ *Small Firms: Setting Up a Business.*

◆ *Small Firms: Employing Staff.*

◆ *Small Firms: Health and Safety.*

Also of help from the Health and Safety Executive (www.hse.gov.uk or www. hsebooks.co.uk):

◆ *Health and Safety Executive: Working with Employers.*

◆ *Managing Health and Safety.*

◆ *Planning for Health and Safety when Selecting and Using Catering Equipment in the Workplace.*

◆ *The Main Health and Safety Law Applicable to Catering.*

9

Marketing

Marketing is one of the most important aspects of your business to get right. You need to give a clear, concise message. It also pays to keep on examining your strategies and re-evaluating your strengths – and weaknesses.

Making marketing a priority

The market is steadily becoming more sophisticated and the number of good restaurants to choose from continues to increase. You need to stand out from the crowd. It isn't enough to sit back and think that your place will pull customers in without some extensive marketing on your part. This is where the first time restaurateur can become unstuck. Get a strategy, allocate funding and do your homework.

You may find your time is taken up with just running your new business once you've started. If you are the sole person the business relies on to do most of the main tasks, it can be very hard, but you will need to sell your business, so factor time in to do this.

You aren't the only salesperson, however. Your front of house staff are equally important in growing your business – and their jobs – so involve them in the process of getting your message across to customers.

This chapter covers:

◆ Identifying your market.

◆ Choosing a name.

◆ Advice on signage.

◆ Business cards.

◆ Stationery.

◆ Menu design.

◆ Web pages.

◆ Advertising.

◆ Launching yourself into the market.

◆ Getting a media profile.

◆ Other business expansion ideas.

◆ Guides profiles.

◆ How to enhance your lunchtime trade through marketing.

Identifying your target market

This is vital. You need to identify your customers' ages, incomes and occupations and local businesses. Then identify your customer needs – business lunches, quick set pre-theatre meals and Sunday evening openings which may be an untapped market, for example.

Look at the competition and what attracts customers to other restaurants, what their strengths are and their market share. Is there a reason why there are few restaurants in the area? If so, examine why.

Finally think about the trends – changes in local tourism, lifestyle changes and population shifts – to give you further customer targeting information.

There are various ways to get this information including:

◆ the business section of a good, local library;

◆ tourism authorities;

◆ your local Business Link office;

◆ local commerce or traders' groups;

◆ professional market research services;

◆ prospective customers, restaurant staff and suppliers.

> *The over 50s hold 40% of the nation's disposable income with 15 million people over the age of 50 in the UK (Age Concern 2006). With shrewd marketing, you can capture a lucrative share of this discerning, loyal market.*

Choosing a name

Do you see your gastropub or brasserie as a neighbourhood one, a destination one or a passing trade business? The name is all-important to attract the type of customer you want to enter your doors.

What messages are you sending out with rather questionable names such as Kitch 'n D'Or (oh, yes, it exists), Bizarre Bazaar, Thai Tanic, Cup 'O' Chino and Kwizeen (they do too)? I suggest not very professional ones. It does depend on your market, of course. Choose a name which fits your aims and personality.

Don't choose too bland a name that no one remembers, nor a complicated, tongue-twisting one which you struggle with when answering the phone. Your business name is a vital word-of-mouth marketing tool, and you will not gain if customers can't pronounce the name to pass on to their friends and colleagues.

Should you be fortunate enough to have a property by a river, capitalise on the location by calling it *The Brasserie On The Bridge* or equivalent. This does draw people to you who read the guides, write-ups and advertising, always on the lookout for a restaurant with a good view. But call it appropriately, and only if there is a view of the water (in this instance). A feeling of being had won't win over new custom. Do avoid cliché names.

Your signage

The sign you have outside your business can have a huge impact. It is vital to make first impressions count. Never skimp on a professional sign-maker's expertise and make your own signs unless you have the gift. If you come across a sign in your area which appeals, find out from the business who the sign-maker is.

Choose an unfussy, readable font to promote your business, and match the design and font to your other promotional material. Match the sign to your building: if it's modern, do modern; if it's Georgian, avoid going Gothic. Keep it simple. Light the signs. Consider carefully the background colour and the colour of the lettering so it creates the right impact and is easy to read. One poorly made sign of dark red with black lettering in my area is illegible: the business has shot itself in the foot before even opening its doors. Add the number of the street in lettering large enough to be seen by a passing car. Could your business benefit from several signs for customers approaching from more than one direction?

If you have a gate, fence or wall by the entry to your premises and use any of these to place your signs on, make sure that bushes and other foliage don't obstruct the signs.

Contact your local authority for permission for signage and lighting prior to having the sign made. It may not be passed due to size, colour or lighting, so play safe.

Signage within your business, too, may be necessary. For professionalism, it may be advisable to pass on the cutesy 'boys, lads' and 'girls, lasses' room approach which many customers find wince-making.

Contact the local authority for brown signs to which you may be entitled. This signage can have a good effect on your business.

Promotional material

Promotional material can include business cards, printed paper, flyers, menus, sample menus to take away, newsletter and website. Depending on the type and size of business you may not wish to have all the above promotional material, but some will be obvious necessities. Decide what is necessary for you. A small restaurant may only need business cards and can make their own menus and headed paper using a computer. Or a menu board, clearly written, may be your choice.

When designing your material, take the following into account:

◆ Choose a font very carefully. A funky, angular one will merely be difficult to read. A clean, clear one is approachable and inspires confidence. Choose the same font consistently.

◆ Will you have a logo? If so, you could design it yourself, although it is well worth paying a professional to come up with something simple and effective.

Business cards

Make your business cards stand out through design and perhaps colour. Remember to include the name of your business (it has been known to leave it out!), address, complete telephone number, website (if applicable), perhaps bullet points of strengths (fresh local fish, log fires, views of the sea, in a prestigious guide, etc.)

Printed paper

This will be used for letters and notes. Have a heading, registered office (if applicable), address, telephone/fax, email, website and logo.

Compliment slips

These are handy for sending menus or confirmation of a booking or other information by post, but not essential. Position the 'With compliments' to the side or base to leave space for writing a note.

Flyers

Flyers are useful for leaving at various sites, for handing out and for passers-by to take away with them. Include all the relevant information (who, where, what, when open, etc.) plus a sample menu and bullet points of strengths (see business cards). They can be A5 or compliment slip size.

Brochures

Brochures are increasingly being used as a marketing tool by more upmarket restaurants. Add photographs, sample menus and information with opening times, a map and, perhaps, information about private dining facilities, car park facilities, outside dining or bar areas. They are rarely used by gastropubs or small brasseries, however.

A big 'don't do' in my book is photography of smiling people, usually models, who look like the cat's pyjamas as they gaze at one another over a perfectly groomed table awash with lobster tails and stemmed glasses, but not like real people really enjoying themselves at **your** restaurant. You don't wish to alienate customers either by inferring you only cater for models or a younger crowd.

Menus

Menus are best kept simple with the name of the restaurant as a heading. Options include printed ones if the menu varies little or seasonally, hand-written (clearly) or computer-printed ones if the menu is small and changes more regularly.

Thanks to the computer, it is easy to create your menus and print them off on a when-needed basis. Do check menus constantly and discard those that are marked or bent. If choosing covers for menus or wine lists, check that they are also handed out to customers scrupulously clean and unmarked. A dirty menu gives out the wrong impression immediately and may indicate a less than sparklingly clean, hygienic business. Similarly, a menu with spelling mistakes does not give the impression of a professionally-run restaurant.

Sample menus are an excellent marketing device. Don't forget to include the name of the restaurant and other relevant information. Have these, flyers and business cards accessible and replenish the space taken up by these marketing tools regularly.

Newsletters

These are a great way of keeping regular customers informed of local and calendar events with suggestions of menus to match the event or time of year. Or you can offer a special menu that ties in with a tight schedule, menu changes, new produce, a range of wines new to the list or a celebration of the first year of opening.

Newsletters can be as personal or restrained as befits your market, and allow you to keep your business in your customers' thoughts – a mail out often results in bookings or enquiries.

Website

Customers are increasingly looking to the Internet for information, a website is a boon for business. It is relatively cheap, and good for small businesses which have a minimal marketing budget.

The traffic to your site is dependent not only on your including the website address on your promotional materials but also on search engines which will make your marketing even more productive. Searchers will either have your website address or may key in one word or one group of words such as 'restaurants in Winchester'.

Research other people's websites and either design it yourself or choose a designer whose work appeals to you. Look at a variety of websites for design inspiration. Get several quotes before committing yourself. Ask about the success of the designer's work, for example how many hits the website attracts. Choose the background colour with care so that the website is readable. Some designers can be too ambitious or funky.

Include on your website:

◆ who to contact;
◆ what your business offers;
◆ sample menus or full menus;
◆ drinks list;
◆ times and days of opening;
◆ how to book a table;
◆ a map;
◆ photographs of the restaurant's exterior (if it merits it) and of the interior.

Keep the website updated and either do the upkeep yourself or agree on a monthly/retainer fee with the web designer. Above all, keep it simple and easily navigable. A static website, i.e. one which doesn't change or update, can send out the wrong signals and can arguably be worse than no website at all as it may demonstrate a slack approach.

> *Don't try to make yourself look up to date and add a sham website address to your promotional material. People will look for it and if it doesn't exist this will give a very bad impression.*

Put yourself in the shoes of the potential customer. Is your website welcoming, practical and professional-looking and geared towards the customers whom you would like to attract?

Advertising

To advertise or not to advertise – in the local press or in appropriate national publications – that is the question.

Look through your local papers and you will see the same restaurants' advertisements. Christmas, Mothering Sunday and Bank Holidays bring out a rash of ads, too, from low to middle range or chain restaurants, rarely from those who aim to offer top quality food and service. These ads tend to offer Meal Deals, the menus often identical, with kids' food at vastly reduced prices.

In my experience as a restaurateur of a small, independent upmarket country restaurant, it simply doesn't pay to advertise in the local papers. It is far more effective to use other marketing skills to get your message across: via *Yellow Pages*, media relationships, guide books, mail shots, a newsletter, handouts, website, Internet and local tourism publications. Word of mouth is one of your most effective marketing tools. It has been estimated one satisfied customer tells between five and ten people about their experience.

If you do decide to advertise, look carefully at your local newspapers to see which of them target your audience. You can obtain a media profile from your local publications which will give you a lot of research information. But make sure it is up to date. Look at the website, www.jicreg.co.uk (Joint Industry Committee for Regional Press Research) to gauge the readership statistics of the majority of UK newspapers.

Ask pertinent questions when contacting the advertising department:

◆ What is the circulation?

◆ What is the readership – age groups, for example, and standard socio-economic categories:

　◆　A = higher managerial, administrative or professional;

　◆　B = intermediate managerial, administrative or professional;

- C1 = junior managerial, administrative or professional;
- C2 = skilled manual workers;
- D = semi- and un-skilled manual workers;
- E = those at the lowest level of subsistence.
- Ask what the shopping patterns of their readership are (taking holidays abroad, buying new cars, etc.)
- Are the papers free, or do the readers pay for them?
- If it's a daily paper what is the best day to place your ad? It might well be best placed on the entertainments page, for example, which only comes out on, say, Thursdays.
- Which is the best section for your ad? Always stipulate where you would like your ad to be placed (if it appears in an inappropriate page, ask for it to be reprinted at no charge).
- See a copy of your ad beforehand to agree it, and proof-read it thoroughly.
- Equally, look at local magazines and ask the same questions.

Other ways of advertising – paid and free – include:

- *Yellow Pages*.
- Posters.
- Local tourism publications.
- Local Tourist Information offices or Visitor Information Service websites who may have an eating out list.
- Direct mail.
- Newsletters for promotions, seasonal information, menus, staff changes, etc.
- Internet (look at your area for online restaurant sites).
- Brochures and programmes for sporting events.
- Brochures and programmes for festivals, theatres, art galleries, art house cinemas and the like.

Advertorials

This is a mix of public relations and advertising. You agree to place a set number of advertisements and in return you get a glowing report of your restaurant written by you and the advertising department. You will be persuaded to take a series of ads. It also includes a picture of your business.

The advertorial may include a visit by a staff member to have a meal at your restaurant; the style of the place, the menu, wine list and service all end up with a 100% recommendation. This fools no one and is a very cheesy way of advertising, in my view, and best avoided if you are aiming at a good, discerning clientele.

Advertising nationally/internationally

You may wish to advertise in specialist interest magazines if your restaurant is in an area of outstanding natural beauty, a boating, or a walking or hill-climbing area, for example. You might be in an historic or cultural city too. Search out publication guides such as *Willings*, *Benn's Media Guide*, *BRAD* (*British Rate and Data*) at your local library to research these magazines. You will also find out advertising rates and how to contact them.

Advertising wording

Your advertisement is selling your business so it must:
◆ grab the reader's attention (a heading, a picture);
◆ stimulate interest (menu suggestions, specialist wines or beers);
◆ plant the idea firmly in the head of the reader that this may be the place they are looking for (value for money or quality of food, the latter locally produced and well-sourced, for example);
◆ be concise and give out the appropriate information – who you are, where you are, what you are offering, how you can be contacted.

> *If your restaurant is in the Good Food Guide or any of the better guides, put this information in your ad. However, the Michelin forbids mention.*

At the same time, it's important to avoid:
◆ being pushy, arrogant or personal ('don't look any further. . . . ');
◆ bragging ('we are by far the best gastropub in the area');

◆ using flowery language ('a tian of Mediterranean vegetables perfumed by rose petals');

◆ contravening the Trades Descriptions Act by offering something you can't deliver ('we offer organic fresh salmon sourced from the Galapagos Islands').

Other advertising tips

◆ If you have taken over someone else's business there may be an existing advertising contract. Do re-evaluate this.

◆ When people book, ask them how they heard about your restaurant and keep this information to help you gauge the effectiveness of advertising.

◆ Don't respond to a cold call from a sales person offering advertising. They will always try to persuade you with a must-have special offer or deal. Either ignore the call as politely as possible or ask them to send you details and then check the publication to see if the expense is worthwhile.

◆ Do stick to your budget.

Other marketing tips

◆ If you plan to offer a discounted or good-value lunch, target retirement establishments and sheltered housing to distribute or leave menus and flyers in lobbies, if permitted, or in lobbies of community centres and other similar places. Lunch is a booming part of business as more and more retired people prefer to lunch and drive/walk home in daylight.

◆ Leave a slip of paper for recruiting names and addresses from customers on tables or enclose it with the bill. You can then remind them of your business with a mail shot of a new menu or special events. If you ask for your customers' email addresses (and gain permission to contact them) you can easily send them information about your latest menus or special offers for no cost – other than your own time.

◆ Make sure you get your restaurant's phone number and address in the *Yellow Pages* and in the telephone directory. You can, of course, put an advertisement in the *Yellow Pages* too.

Your media profile

What message do you wish to send out to the media (radio, television, the press) if you are keen to attract attention this way? Recognise what your unique strengths are and what you are offering the public – and the media you would like to woo – before you can decide how to attract them.

What is your style? Is it purely culinary? Purely looks? Based purely on the character of the owner and or chef? Ideally it's a mix of all three. An independent restaurateur must find his or her own voice and own style to project, to sell to the media.

Before touting for new business via media coverage, you must believe in yourself and be committed to be able to offer what you say you can offer. Can you deliver the goods? What makes you unique? What makes people want to contact you?

How to get media coverage

Achieving media coverage via the people who work for you is one way. For example:

◆ You have just taken on a high-profile chef or one with an interesting pedigree or background.

◆ Your sommelier has worked in a high-profile place.

◆ A member of staff has an unusual background.

◆ Your produce is sourced from an unusual supplier or is unusual in itself.

◆ Your building is historic, or renovated to high standard, or is on an interesting site.

◆ You have changed from being a commercial city high-flyer, or nun, to open a restaurant in the area.

◆ Your restaurant has changed hands after 20 years of ownership by a much-loved character, a local personality, for example.

Top tips for getting media coverage

◆ **Do some research**. Look at newspapers, magazines, radio and television at your local library. Ask your librarian for help with available publications. Also, consider reading/buying *The Guardian Media Guide*, and researching useful guides, such as *Willings and Benn's*.

◆ **Make a media list**. This should include local and national newspapers, magazines, local and national radio programmes, trade magazines with contact numbers and emails where possible.

◆ **Send a press release**. First, phone to find out whom to contact and get the correct spelling of their name. Send them a press release (see below on how to write one) with a photograph of the interior, the chef, a dish, the new owner, for example. Be sure to send it to the right person.

> *Should you call after sending a press release? Journalists are incredibly busy and some find it a distinct irritant to be called. Others don't. If calling, phone them within a week or ten days of sending the release.*

◆ Contact magazine-style radio programme presenters who do interviews, to see if you can be interviewed. Send a press release and some background to your business to spark an interest first.

◆ It pays to keep your media list up to date and to talk or send a press release on a regular basis to keep your business in the public eye. Keep any communication professional, short and newsworthy

Writing a press release

Press releases can be an excellent tool for business promotion if they are properly written and presented. They are not a page-long ad, nor are they a novel. Neither are they a promotional piece full of detail. They are concise, to the point and newsworthy, and they tell a short story, or relate an event, with clarity.

Be sure to read the publication you are targeting before sending the press release. Do some homework and visit the publication's website and look at the style, the content and, if possible, buy the publication. This means you will be able to understand the readers' needs and get a better response from your press release.

Write with the targeted journalist in mind: he or she is not looking to buy your product or service, but to fill a news need. So when you are writing, ask the question, 'Why should readers care about A, B or C?' rather than 'What's in it for me?' Start with an bold heading encapsulating your reasons for sending it.

For example:

Saffron Aitkin, Gordon Ramsay protegée to join Le Minou Brasserie, Bristol as head chef

Develop the press release with newsworthy items, such as what strengths Saffron will bring to the brasserie due to her culinary style and background. Saffron may be hosting a sample menu tasting or she may be holding a charity promotion or offering cookery courses.

Finally, add other details:

Notes for editor: *Le Minou Brasserie*, owned and run by Sam Waterford, opened in 1999, is in the *Good Food Guide* and has two rosettes in the *AA Guide*. For further information and for photography contact Sam Waterford – [with full contact details].

Golden rules of writing press releases

◆ Use headed paper with contact name, address, phone, email.

◆ Print **Press Release** at top of release.

◆ Prominently display date of press release.

◆ Then put 'For immediate publication' or 'embargoed to July 1' (if there is a reason for keeping the news until a later date) also at the top.

◆ Choose your font carefully. It must be easily readable and not quirky.

◆ Put the text in double spacing or small paragraphs divided by a space.

◆ Keep it short. One page between 400–500 words.

◆ If you must go onto another page, don't use the back of the page but a new sheet.

◆ Always finish with 'ENDS'.

◆ Send press releases by post for maximum impact. Emails are quickly deleted but some might work.

Critics

Don't confuse advertorials with critics, the former part of the advertising process with a staff member of the newspaper writing a glowing report of your restaurant, the latter an unsolicited review by a professional reviewer of your restaurant who will come unannounced and unbidden.

If you believe in your restaurant then you will welcome a critic. However, you will only welcome a critic who understands the restaurant business and not necessarily a celebrity reviewer who may be simply out for him or herself with little knowledge, understanding or interest in the business. Such reviewers are usually attention-seeking and have little respect within the restaurant industry. Restaurants generally deserve much better than the reviews these people give.

Critics can be vicious but can equally heap praise on where praise is due.

I must declare my interest: I am a restaurant critic and restaurant inspector and have been for a number of years. I was a chef and restaurant owner. Not all critics need to have this background, of course, but it is immensely useful to have been steeped in the business before taking up the critical pen.

Some restaurateurs grumble – after a poor review – that the critic is not an ordinary customer. Good critics see themselves as just this but, perhaps, with a more discerning eye. Criticism must be based on the food, sourcing of produce, the kitchen's skills, front of house staff, the degree of care and attention shown to the customer and the degree of comfort with at least a decent chair to sit on rather than one that cuts into the backs of your legs. Yes, even in a gastropub.

It is not purely the food the critic has to focus on, however, but also the feel of the restaurant and if the experience was a successful, enjoyable one. A good critic is aware of hospitality, creativity, innovation and any theatrical buzz that may be present.

Negative criticism is useless unless the writer can give reasons as to why the food, atmosphere or service was poor. It is simply not good enough to say, 'I didn't like my pork belly with pak choi'. Why not? Was it tough, too salty, the meat poorly sourced, the vegetable wildly overcooked? A critic owes it to the restaurant to explain why.

Critics do have the power to close a business. Their judgement can be that tough on businesses. I have done so and derive no pleasure from it, apart from saving people money by not eating there. Some restaurateurs are simply not cut out to be in the business and do great damage to the reputation of the industry.

On the positive side, a good critique of a restaurant can create boom time, the phone ringing non-stop for bookings. If this happens to you, give the critic a call or send a card. It is always appreciated.

Getting a bad review

Ultimately, your customers are your best critics but if there is a shift down in numbers coming through your door it may be time to reappraise your efforts. If a review was bad and you respect the writer for their style, understanding and fair points, then you must take it on board and resolve to address the criticism.

There will always be times in the life of a restaurant when not everything runs smoothly: your chef burns a hand, a staff member hasn't removed the lipstick from a just-washed glass and a late meat delivery results in too little time to prep properly. You will just have to accept the negative press reaction should the critic be in that evening. But it is simply no good relying on 'chef's night off' as an excuse. If the chef was off, the deputy has to achieve the same standards. Or close the restaurant that day/evening.

But, if your restaurant has little in the way of commendation and is purely PR hype without substance and you get a real roasting, then it's time to re-evaluate your goals.

National and regional critics

National critics respected by restaurateurs and the public alike include Fay Maschler (*London Evening Standard*) and Jay Rayner (*Observer*). They know their onions and can deliver some pretty savage blows as well as praise. The ones not to take seriously include Michael Winner (*Sunday Times*). Be very wary of approaching others such as AA Gill (*Sunday Times*) as he and others are the Rottweilers of the genre.

If you do approach any restaurant critic with information about your restaurant in the hope that you will get a write-up, make sure you do so with your eyes wide open. It is a long shot that your restaurant will be chosen for a write-up by national papers. Many critics stay in town, only occasionally venturing outside of London.

However, regional newspapers that have a review column welcome any reports of a new restaurant opening or change of chef and, if they are worth their salt, will do an anonymous write-up rather than accept an invitation to be your guest. I am always very pleased to know of changes in my area of Hampshire and West Sussex and will put names on my list of restaurants to review. In common with national critics I will never go as a guest as it could be seen as compromising my objectivity.

The guides

There are good, mediocre and bad guides. I list the ones that matter in the trade, the ones that restaurateurs aspire to achieve an entry in rather than the guides that you pay to have an entry.

Top guides, as recognised by restaurateurs and customers, are *The Good Food Guide* and *The Michelin Guide in the UK and Ireland*. Other good guides include the *AA Restaurant Guide*, *Eating Out in Pubs* (Michelin), *Harden's UK Restaurants* (although not a favourite of many restaurateurs), *Time Out Eating and Drinking in Great Britain and Ireland*, *Time Out Eating and Drinking In London* and Georgina Campbell's *Jameson Guide Ireland*. *The Zagat Survey* can also be useful. Do submit your restaurant with details, menu, wine list, how to find you and covering letter in the hope that an inspector may come calling.

The Good Food Guide

First published in 1952, then taken up and published by the *Which? Consumers Guides* in 1962, *The Good Food Guide* is the one found in keen diners' cars for reference when searching for a recommended restaurant or pub.

Raymond Postgate, the first editor, created the first stocky little pocket edition in those post-war years, inspectors recruited including a future Chancellor of the Exchequer, three world-famous English conductors, a socialist bishop and John Arlott, the cricket commentator. Editors have included Christopher Driver, Drew Smith, Tom Jaine and Jim Ainsworth.

The GFG continues to be very much a compendium of shared experiences by readers and inspectors, this shared wealth of knowledge covering 1,000 main entries and 300 in a round-up section of England, Wales, Scotland, Northern Ireland, the Republic of Ireland and the Channel Islands' best on offer.

There are currently 70 inspectors nationally and they are the eyes and ears on the ground. They are freelance, keep the guide informed of what's going on in their area and undertake official yet anonymous visits on behalf of the guide.

Some have professional experience in the hospitality industry as either chefs or restaurateurs; others are food and wine journalists. Readers' reports are also part of the guide's makeup.

The Good Food Guide, a very readable, unfussy, user-friendly publication with easy to follow symbols and good layout, is published yearly in October.

Restaurants are not charged for inclusion in the guide. Contact the guide by sending in menus, wine list and information about your restaurant and staff and an inspection may follow.

Contact: www.which.net

The AA Restaurant Guide

With over 1,800 restaurants awarded rosettes by the AA's professional inspectors, the latest edition has at last been revamped with clearer content design and more detail. Rosetted restaurants are inspected annually, and feature purely on merit with no charge for inclusion. A full page is given to each 4- and 5-rosetted restaurant, plus a half-page entry for every 3-rosette award. There are 4 AA Wine Awards, with 100 notable wine list symbols awarded to the runners up. It also includes the AA Restaurant of the Year Awards and AA Seafood and Wine Awards. It does focus on British and European cooking rather than ethnic restaurants.

AA rosettes are awarded solely for the cooking and consistency, the standard to be achieved 'regardless of the chef's day off!' Ambience, style, comfort, layout and presentation of menu, appearance, attitude and efficiency of service and the quality of the wine list 'should all fit the ambition of the cooking' too. There are other entries too for non-rosette winners.

There is no payment required for entry but pictures cost. The editor welcomes restaurants to submit their details for inspection and, hopefully, inclusion.

Contact: www.theaa.com

The AA Pub Guide

Billed as 'the UK's best selling full-colour Pub Guide', it is the sister publication to the Restaurant Guide and has also undergone a welcome design change for easier reading. It features recommended pubs in Britain recognised for their quality and atmosphere and includes 2,000 ancient taverns, traditional countryside inns, gastro-pubs and hostelries, selected on merit with no charge for inclusion. Also featured is AA inspected and rated accommodation. Quality seafood pubs are highlighted. There are also useful symbols throughout, AA Rosettes, Stars & Diamonds and Wine Glasses showing wines available by the glass, plus AA Pub of the Year Awards and AA Seafood Pub of the Year Awards.

Michelin Eating Out in Pubs

A sister publication of the Michelin Guide, this guide highlights around 600 of the best pubs serving good food in the UK and Ireland. Derek Bulmer, the editor, says: 'With so many additions this year [2007] the gastropub phenomenon shows no sign of abating, particularly in the south and east of England where growth has been strongest. Another welcome trend is the increasing use of local produce which more and more pubs proudly promote.'

Chosen pubs have been selected for the quality of their cooking but several are deserving of special mention.

The guide features an in-depth description and colour photograph, and there is information on typical dishes and specialities, the beer they serve, including real ales, and symbols to denote particularly interesting wine lists and choice of wines by the glass. Other essential information includes opening times and prices, directions and driving distances from local towns and details of accommodation where available.

Contact: www.viamichelin.com

The Michelin Guide

The Michelin Guide, conceived in France in 1900 for hungry motorists, now has eight guides covering 21 European countries, the UK title having been first published in 1974. It covers hotels and restaurants with minimal wording, its timeless symbols denoting facilities, features and categories.

The guide, published annually, employs only 70 full-time inspectors for the whole of Europe who have training and experience in the hotel and catering industry. Each establishment 'is visited and/or tested by our staff at least once in the year' including many that don't make the grade.

This is the guide many chefs aspire to, a Michelin star adding huge kudos firstly to the chef and secondly to the restaurant. If the chef decamps, the star is lost to both chef and restaurant. Brasseries and gastropubs can aspire to having a Michelin star or being in the *Michelin Eating Out in Pubs Guide*.

◆ **Three Michelin stars**: 'Exceptional cuisine, worth a special journey – one always eats here extremely well, sometimes superbly. Fine wines, faultless service, elegant surroundings. One will pay accordingly.'

◆ **Two Michelin stars**: 'Excellent cooking, worth a detour – specialities and wines of first class quality. This will be reflected in the price.'

◆ **One Michelin star**: 'A very good restaurant in its category. The star indicated a good place to stop on your journey. But beware of comparing the star given to an expensive 'de luxe' establishment to that of a simple restaurant where you can appreciate fine cooking at a reasonable price.'

Other restaurant symbols include crossed knives and forks – one to five – which denote the degree of comfort, the latest addition being a fork and mug for traditional pubs serving good food.

The *Bib Gourmand*, the Michelin man head in red, denotes good food at moderate prices at a less elaborate restaurant, brasserie or gastropub.

In the past, it was perceived that, in order to gain a star, lavish comfort was one irrefutable necessity. This has been relaxed quite considerably due to changing, more relaxed times. Two pubs, unthinkable only several years ago, have been awarded stars in the latest guide.

A Michelin inspector (now ex) recently wrote a controversial book about the guide, stating that the gourmet restaurant bible was understaffed, out of date and in thrall to big-name chefs in France. A number of restaurateurs and critics were not surprised by these criticisms as they had felt the guide had lost some of its authority. Despite this, it is still seen by many as a true reflection of good restaurants (and hotels) in the 21 countries featured in the eight published guides. Inclusion is free. The UK Guide is published in mid January.

Contact: www.themichelinguide-gbirl@uk.michelin.com

Georgina Campbell's The Guide – The best places to eat, drink and stay

Georgina Campbell, indefatigable writer on Irish cuisine and hospitality, conceived this guide in 1998. It covers over 1,250 restaurants, pubs, country houses, hotels, cafés, guesthouses and farmhouses throughout the north and south of Ireland and prides itself on highlighting the quality and the variety of Irish produce.

It is particularly interested in restaurants giving the provenance of their ingredients on menus, the emphasis on quality from artisan producers.

The no-gimmick, verbose guide, written with heart-and-soul, has a rating system with a quirky demi-star denoting a restaurant approaching full star status, with three stars being the highest rating. It rightly celebrates the culinary revolution that has taken place in Ireland over the past twenty years.

There is a sister guide, *Georgina Campbell's Ireland: The Dublin Guide* which lists restaurants by post code (as does the main guide in the capital) and by cuisine and speciality. Both assess entries independently and there is no payment for inclusion. No advertising is allowed by entries.

Contact: www.ireland-guide.com

Harden's UK Restaurants

One of the simpler, easier-to-read guide to 'where real people eat', it includes restaurants, country house hotels, pubs, curry houses and chippies, and 'pulls no punches,' according to its editors. Its motto is simple: 'We tell it as it is'.

Published in October each year, Harden's relies on a comprehensive survey of regular restaurant-goers and analyses around 80,000 reports for the guide's 1,500 restaurants.

Categories on the survey include, 'top gastronomic experience', 'your favourite restaurant', 'best bar/pub food', 'most romantic', 'most disappointing cooking' and several other ethnic and cuisine categories. Their rating is 1 to 5 (1 being excellent, 5 being disappointing).

Remy Martin, sponsors of the guide, award Restaurant Remies to new and up and coming restaurants with ten each in London and outside the capital.

No fee is payable for inclusion in this guide or its sister guide, *Harden's London Restaurants* (published in September), nor is any advertising or hospitality accepted.

Also included in both guides are forthcoming openings of note with a brief, non-critical entry outlining contact details. The deadline for submissions is early July for the London restaurants and early August for UK ones.

Harden's Guides were conceived in 1992 (the London guide) and 1998 (UK guide) by brothers Richard and Peter Harden, and has 'an enviable knack of getting the verdict right in as few words as possible' says *Scotland On Sunday*'s restaurant critic. The *Irish Times* goes one better: 'Utterly and ruthlessly honest'. But, a number of restaurateurs have an aversion to this one.

Contact: www.hardens.com

Time Out Eating and Drinking in Great Britain and Ireland and *The Time Out London Eating and Drinking Guide*

The London guide, first published in 1983, was followed by the Great Britain and Ireland edition in 2004 with currently around 1,200 entries in each well-produced, independent publication. These are the books that are the most helpful and readable and come from the large *Time Out* stable of guides.

In the London guide, restaurants are considerately grouped into types and ethnicity of restaurants (brasserie, pubs, wine bars, Greek, Italian, Thai for example), also eating on a budget and by area. There is also a useful, innovative list of which establishments provide brunch and Sunday lunch and which are suitable for late eating, eating alone, taking a date, taking the kids, spotting a celeb, finding the unfamiliar and loving the look.

A red star denotes a very good restaurant of its type, a green star helping to identify a more budget-conscious eatery. Annual awards are given for best bar, pub, local restaurant, brasserie, gastropub, family restaurant, Indian restaurant, cheap eat, vegetarian meal, design, new restaurant and there is also an award for outstanding achievement.

The Time Out Eating and Drinking in Great Britain and Ireland is a very welcome addition to the national scene and uses the same star system and other helpful information. Regional listings include London.

Around 50 'mostly' freelance inspectors, mainly food journalists, are their writers. No payment is required for entry into either book.

Contact: www.timeout.com

The Zagat Survey

Started by New Yorkers Tim and Nina Zagat in 1979 there has been a London restaurant guide for years. It is just one of the many guides in the US and Europe to have emerged via the survey which invites diners to rate and review the restaurants they have visited – and many other leisure pursuits.

However, this quirky read can become tiresome. It does have a location index, useful 'all day dining', 'breakfast/brunch' and many more categories to look up. Not always up to date and not widely known except for aficionados of the genre.

Contact: www.zagat.com

Other guide websites

www.goodguides.co.uk for the *Good Pub Guide*

www.restaurant-guide.com

www.dine-online.co.uk

www.themobilefoodguide.com

www.tabletop.co.uk

www.5pm.co.uk

> *Personal recommendation accounts for around 75% of deciding on a restaurant to visit with* The Good Food Guide *being the guide chosen above all others.*

Local lists

Your local tourist information office may have a list of restaurants and pubs to which you can add your premises. Also scout around the web to link your restaurant to your area. There may also be other websites you can be part of.

Do contact the local media via a press release if you are entered in a prestigious guide (see how to write a press release) and the national media if you have been awarded a Michelin star, an AA rosette or are given a rating in *The Good Food Guide*.

Business expansion

There are slack times in the restaurant trade caused by season or geography. Think, therefore, of adding some extra strings to your bow like cookery classes, outside catering, takeaway, writing for a local or national magazine or newspaper or targeting the corporate market with special lunch deals.

Cookery classes

When is your least busy period? Just after Christmas? The dark days of autumn or winter? Are you a communicator? Capitalise on your premises and your profession to create a series of cookery classes and/or demonstrations. These can be instead of a lunch trade one day (choose a slack day) every month or when the restaurant has its weekly closing day.

What to do:

◆ Write to your customers via a newsletter, put up posters and distribute flyers in the restaurant, in libraries, shops and elsewhere in your area. Outline a series of classes for six or more paying students (it generally won't pay to have fewer) depending on your kitchen size.

◆ Design the classes carefully around your own prep time, leaving plenty of time to clear up, have some time off and prepare for the evening.

◆ Plan the cooking with a domestic kitchen in mind and don't use hard-to-find ingredients. Don't be too technically advanced or you may lose your students. Do have a member of staff in to wash up during the class and help prep before the students' arrival and put this cost into your budget.

◆ Possible timetable No 1:
9.30 am: arrive; coffee and talk.
10 am: start students cooking a two course meal (or whatever you have chosen to do).
12.30: lunch with a glass of wine in restaurant.
2 pm: discussion of cooking and Q & A.
3.30 pm: departure with pack containing recipes, restaurant menus, public relations information.

◆ Possible timetable No 2:
10 am: arrival and coffee.
Demonstration: 11 am – 12.30 pm. Glass of wine with food cooked either still in kitchen or informally in the restaurant.
1.30 pm: leave with tips and recipe pack plus menu and PR.

◆ Offer gift vouchers for classes and demonstrations.

Types of classes

These could be daily, 2–3 day courses, weekly, occasional or seasonal courses. They might offer:

◆ The basics: soups, breads, pâtés, roasts, simple desserts, jams, biscuits.

◆ Cooking for family and friends: simple oven dishes using chicken or pasta.

◆ Cooking lunch: your paying clients cook from scratch and eat the meal in the restaurant with a good glass of wine.

◆ Food from Morocco, Spain, Italy, France, Thailand, Mexico with each country covered in a series of hands-on cooking classes or demonstrations.

◆ Cooking with spices and chillies.

◆ Cooking fish (for example, learning how to skin and fillet fish), meat, game, shellfish, vegetables.

◆ Pasta Day (learning how to make pasta and sauces).

◆ Men in the Kitchen Day.

◆ Entertaining at Home Day.

◆ Vegetarian Day.

◆ Tapas Day.

◆ Simple starters.

◆ Party desserts.

◆ Party buffets.

◆ Party canapés.

◆ How to get through Christmas as the family cook.

◆ Demo Masterclass by the restaurant's chef(s).

◆ Local celebrity chef/food writer demonstration.

The most popular cookery courses are Christmas, Men, Children and Entertaining, but other subjects can easily grab the imagination if presented well and clearly on paper. Calculate your costs carefully before deciding on a price per person. Offer discounts for group bookings: for example, one comes free if he or she books six friends. Make sure your classes measure up to expectations: don't promise more than you can fulfil. Ask your students to fill in a questionnaire before departure for feedback. You may be surprised how much good market research you can achieve.

Outside catering

Your kitchen is an obvious place to capitalise on its assets as well as your skills and those of your staff. You may be able to offer your restaurant customers and others who you target a full year-round outside catering service if you have enough space, equipment and staff. Suggestions:

◆ Do work out carefully what the staff and space can handle.

◆ Plan your outside catering menus around these constraints.

◆ Make a supply list, a work schedule, plan transportation and staffing.

◆ Communication is everything with the client. Failure to do this may jeopardise the party and your reputation.

◆ The day after the party can also mean clearing up and sorting out equipment.

◆ Don't jeopardise your business by taking on too much too soon.

◆ If you decide to do outside catering or takeaway service have printed catering menus for customers to pick up.

◆ Open accounts with companies for breakfasts, lunches, special events or takeaway trade with provisos such as payment terms of 30 days, trade references and stipulate a minimum order and a 24-hour cancellation notice.

Corporate lunches

Service, service, service can often supersede location, location, location thanks to a fast turnaround at lunchtime in the restaurant trade. Business lunches need to be snappy and well managed. It is, therefore, worthy of consideration to attract this market should your restaurant be in close proximity to a number of large or medium-sized businesses.

◆ Draw up a list of businesses in the area.

◆ Contact the administration or human resources department and find out a name to write to.

◆ Prepare a welcoming letter outlining what you can offer the company at lunchtime or for other corporate entertaining either at your restaurant or at the business.

◆ Offer them special discounts which the company can promote on their internal website.

◆ Discuss with your chef (or you may be the chef) the type of dishes that can be offered with swiftness and good value in mind.

◆ Prepare some sample menus and send them with the welcoming letter to the member of staff you have located, adding business cards and copies of good reviews or testimonials from other companies.

♦ Cold starters and desserts are obvious choices that can be quickly plated.

♦ Simply-cooked main courses such as grilled fish, meat and pasta are ideal. A simple plate of the best charcuterie with pickles and salads are also popular.

♦ A glass of wine or soft drink and coffee are added incentives within the price per person, but beware: if you offer poor quality wine or coffee to keep costs down repeat business may not happen.

♦ A business lunch showcases what your business can offer and therefore can provide excellent marketing.

♦ Set up corporate credit accounts, stipulate a minimum order with 24-hours' notice and a 24-hour cancellation notice to safeguard your business and your blood pressure!

Marketing your lunch trade to the general public

As well as trying to get businesses interested, you will also need to look at the local market. Improving lunch sales could be crucial to your business. Some suggestions:

♦ Give discounts and special offer lunches such as good-value cheap two courses.

♦ Offer nearby large company employees special discounts which the company can promote on their internal website.

♦ Contact local clubs and associations to offer them discounts.

♦ Create a special lunch menu at a knock-down price.

♦ Promote your lunch deals by in-house marketing (on menus and cards on tables or by the bar or via a newsletter).

♦ Promote your lunchtime deal via a mailshot or newsletter and give a timed offer.

♦ Keep your lunchtime menu simple and accessible.

♦ Keep on listening to your customers to find out what you might be able to offer them.

Writing a column or a cookbook

These are two excellent means of keeping your restaurant's profile in the media market place. But you must examine your skills and your time. Can you write clearly, concisely and interestingly? Will your column's recipes be user-friendly? Can you fit in the writing as well as cooking and/or running a restaurant? Do you have something offbeat or unusual to impart in a cookbook?

If you believe that you have many of these attributes here are some steps to take:

◆ Contact your local paper, magazine, radio station and talk to the features editor or programme producer about a column.

◆ Write a one-page letter, outlining your book proposal in clear, concise language your culinary attributes and other background which may be of interest – but only if it is relevant. No need to add your 5 A levels, your prowess at mountain walking, your book-binding course …

◆ Go to a good bookshop and look at the cookbooks on offer.

◆ Which books would you like to emulate and why?

◆ Get their publishers' names.

◆ Do you have a good story to tell about your restaurant (grow your own vegetables, herbs and salads, raise chickens for the pot, family-run restaurant for generations, for example)?

◆ Contact the commissioning editors by name either in writing or by phone.

◆ Invest in *The Writer's Handbook* (published by MacMillan, see www.panmacmillan.com) for UK publishers, agents, national and regional newspapers and other useful information or *The Guardian Media Guide* (Atlantic Books) for similar guidance and other media information.

◆ Contact the Guild of Food Writers (www.gfw.co.uk) for advice.

It takes time and perseverance to get on this particular ladder, as I can testify to, but dogged determination can pay off (as I can also testify to!).

Don'ts

◆ Do not write complex recipes that only chefs can aspire to.

◆ Do not write a book unless you have a distinctive, different 'voice'.

◆ Do not take on too much media work – writing a column, a book, TV, radio – as it may take you away from those stoves for too long, your business suffering as a result.

10

Staffing your business

Staff, as most restaurateurs will testify, are both the biggest problem and the biggest asset a business can have.

No matter how good your gastropub or brasserie is, it cannot survive without good staff. Your staff will enhance and reflect the qualities your business offers. Nothing will do more damage to your reputation than having unhelpful, slovenly, couldn't-care-less, rude staff – apart from bad food, that is! Your customers will, rightly, expect them to be consistent, welcoming, calm, knowledgeable and professional.

Temperamental chefs of course exist – and not only on television – but these people are best avoided as no one around them can operate in such an atmosphere. Their attitude rubs off on other staff in the restaurant too, so choose your chefs – and other staff – prudently. Front of house managers can equally be influential.

Verbal, intimidating behaviour and especially physical abuse is not to be tolerated in the kitchen or restaurant. These traits rightly belong to the past.

Is catering unique? Every industry thinks it is unique and in a sense, each is right. This is an unusual industry, with its uniforms, myriad of job titles, tipping, unsocial hours, labour mobility and irregular work flow. These peculiarities and the degree of entrepreneurship needed in the restaurant business amply demonstrate that the catering industry is certainly a special case.

Due to this 'special case' status, one thing is for sure: you must be organised. And that means good staffing at all levels, staff who are flexible, understand the need for speed when busy, but who never compromise on quality. They must have the ability to do other jobs such as cleaning and undergo extra training if necessary during less busy times. Motivation by management is prerequisite for keeping good staff. Job satisfaction cannot be underestimated.

This chapter deals with:

◆ Service.

◆ Staffing problems.

◆ College and agency recruitment, casual and agency staff.

◆ Catering management.

◆ Job descriptions, interviewing.

◆ Explanation of kitchen hierarchy.

◆ Staff organisation and training.

◆ Job details including cleaning rotas, dress code, meals, holidays, smoking, overtime, behaviour.

◆ Pay legalities.

◆ Basic waiting skills and management skills.

◆ Communicating effectively with guests and clients.

The importance of service

Service is central in today's competitive restaurant marketplace. As standards rise in quality produce and comfort, so they must in terms of service which, of course, covers all kitchen, waiting and cleaning staff as well as any other employees in a restaurant business. Personal service and attention to detail set the best restaurants apart from the rest.

We have entered a period of high demand for good staffing as a result of the booming restaurant trade, but this labour supply needs to come from somewhere. Will potential employees be trained sufficiently to offer good service and high standards? This is of concern to all restaurateurs.

There is no doubt that the work is demanding and that it can be seen as a dead end job by some. But, thankfully, others see it as a stimulating and rewarding challenge.

The hospitality industry is sometimes seen as theatre. Some in this profession love to entertain, but they must always remain seriously professional whilst demonstrating humour, good judgement and sensitivity.

Staff need direction, motivation and incentive to carry out their work and also need to be very flexible. Direction, motivation and incentive all come from management. All staff need to be accepted by both sexes, have the ability to make customers feel at ease and to be respected by their employers.

Waiters and waitresses – skilled ones – offer service. They are not servants. They have talked to the kitchen about the composition of the food and are able to advise customers about which combinations go best together if the customer is in doubt. They are aware when and how to clear a table. When to pour wine. When a customer is getting restless for the bill. They are also aware of tips and how to generate this extra income. They must be an asset to your business.

Kitchen staff are creative in different ways. Chefs must have the ability to prepare food and time cooking to a split second with speed and accuracy. They must be able to do it time and time again to the same high standard. Consistency is all. Your head chef needs to know how to source excellent produce and to be able to cook it with passion, skill and care. Apprenticeship is alive and well and should be encouraged vigorously, and many students attend day release courses while working in a restaurant kitchen.

Finding staff

When an employee leaves or you expand your business, finding staff – good, suitable staff – is essential for the good running of your gastropub or brasserie. Consider the type of skills you require and the degree of experience you need. Prospective employees may have sufficient experience, but still need to be trained to your way of doing things. Or they may be new to the business, but willing, and need careful nurturing. Write a job description with necessary and desirable attributes. You may wish to include a summary of the job, outlining the experience, personality, specialist knowledge, training, qualifications and other requirements necessary to your business.

Once you have prepared your specifications, you can either ask current staff if they know of any suitable candidates, advertise on the premises, at your local job centre or elswhere.

Other sources for sourcing good staff include:

◆ recruitment agencies;

◆ existing staff looking for promotion;

◆ waiting list – people coming to the restaurant looking for a job;

◆ previous applicants;

◆ casual callers;

◆ schools and colleges.

Local recruitment

Train local people to deliver the goods. Create a good team by encouraging their creative side, but with good, solid guidelines laid down either by management or by a head chef. Kitchens that work well are by staffed by local people who enjoy being together and creating good food and service.

All staff, either local or not, must be able to cover for one another in time of crisis or staff absence so that the whole service runs smoothly. Never hire whingers, clock watchers or lazy people. These traits could be difficult to assess at interview, granted, but, by judicious questions or by their manner, you may be able to spot them. They can infect a good team.

Catering colleges are one source of kitchen staffing, but the standard in some is questionable, the teaching focusing on hotel-like service which is past its sell-by date, according to employers. Some, however, are excellent. But others still make flour-based sauces, soups and stocks from packets, and heavy, stodgy food which is out of kilter with today's tastes. This is compounded by outmoded silver service (useful, perhaps, for banqueting) and folding napkins into unnecessary shapes, amongst other contentious catering issues.

Some colleges have moved on, thankfully, and are teaching their students the art of lighter cuisine combined with slow cooking (*daubes*, terrines and bread-making for example). They are sourcing their materials with care and attention and teaching their students how to run a kitchen amongst other modern and commercial necessities. These colleges are training the chefs who will be able to deliver the consistently high standards that customers expect and good restaurateurs wish to achieve.

However, some students, when leaving college, sometimes feel they wasted their time as the real world can present quite a different aspect of their chosen profession and they have to start the learning process all over again.

Staff's attitude to food

Restaurant employers are also handicapped by some students' and non-trained staff's backgrounds. The type of food at home can be quite at variance with food offered in restaurants. There can be a mountain to climb in terms of food education, but when a staff member sees the light and becomes excited about the type and quality of the food and service, it's a eureka moment.

This is a bleak outlook I am aware: staffing is a growing problem resulting from a fast-food nation of eaters who know or care little about cooking, or who come from a background of not eating as a family around a table. Some entering the profession see the catering trade as a way to becoming famous – and fast; to follow in the footsteps of the Jamie Olivers of this world without having to work too hard: unlike Jamie, who started from the bottom of the heap and proved himself.

Recruitment agencies

Placing a well-worded advertisement in local papers will sometimes attract the right kind of people. For more permanent staff such as a head chef, you may have to recruit staff through agencies.

Catering agencies are employment agencies dedicated to this specific industry. They may place staff permanently or temporarily. There may be 30,000 vacancies on any one day in London alone as a result of the burgeoning restaurant and hotel market. Job vacancies include head chefs, trainee-, commis- and sous- chefs, kitchen porters, waiters and waitresses, bar staff and managers.

An agency charges at least 10% of the agreed wage.

It is important to weigh up the costs and advantages if recruiting agency staff. On the plus side, many agencies get to know their applicants well and match appropriate chefs to appropriate businesses. It's not in their interests to get this wrong but, of course, it can and does happen, some agencies seeing the chef as merely making money for them. Agencies aren't cheap and you may achieve just as good, if not better results, with an advertisement which may attract greater numbers of applicants.

Temporary agency staff are usually paid per hour. This may cause friction once this is known by your other staff if their hourly rate doesn't match the temp's pay, so try to avoid this, if possible.

Promote from within. It is easier and more cost effective to find a commis chef from an agency rather than going to an agency to recruit a higher position. Your own chef may be able to train up a commis chef to a higher grade.

Agencies' standard hourly rates can be high, and the staff are a mixed bag of excellent, good, poor and dreadful. It can depend on staff the agency itself can recruit, so ask pertinent questions:

◆ What is your hourly rate?
◆ Does this include VAT?
◆ Is there an extra charge for Sunday work?
◆ How much experience do your staff have?
◆ Are they trained or casual labour?
◆ How many hours can they work?
◆ What are your overtime charges?
◆ Can I have only non-smoking staff?
◆ How much importance does your company attach to grooming?
◆ Do you provide them with clothing or guide them on what to wear?
◆ Do they speak English? (Or whatever language you prefer.)
◆ Can I have all the details in writing?

Put your foot down with smoking breaks. Staff who smoke should be encouraged not to take smoking breaks as this unfairly increases the pressure on non-smoking staff. It is also unpleasant for customers to smell smoke on staff members' clothing, hands and breath.

Unskilled staff

What motivates those without skills? Reasons why unskilled catering work is popular are:

◆ the work is easy to learn;

◆ there is variety;

◆ it is not a factory;

◆ you meet people;

◆ it is convenient to have quick money and doesn't have to be permanent.

How to motivate people

It is necessary to introduce good housekeeping practices with staff in order to keep them. This can be achived by:

◆ clear communication. It is not possible to respond positively when there is no clarity;

◆ not over controlling;

◆ recognising achievement. This will result in increased good performance;

◆ good teaching;

◆ rewarding adequately;

◆ reviewing performance on a regular basis;

◆ treating staff like human beings and not like cogs in a machine;

◆ avoiding promises and favours and not delivering them;

◆ taking what people say seriously – listening to staff;

◆ investigating complaints or grievances;

◆ avoiding deals;

◆ making your staff realise they are a team;

◆ recognising a career commitment.

Many people enjoy working in a team. Find things that your staff have in common other than simply working for the same business (e.g., they are all students, all women, all the same age). Work on these shared characteristics and build up the bonds.

Commitment to the job can also be achieved by staff being prepared to ditch old skills and learn new ones. If they are empowered and their assets are recognised, they may well become loyal, flexible and invaluable staff members.

The staff interview

The relationship between employer and employee may start when the manager says 'Start Monday' and the applicant says 'OK'. But what agreement has been reached?

At the interview stage, the interviewer is keen to assess the capabilities of the interviewee regarding effort, general willingness and track record (if not taking on a novice in the business). At that 'Start Monday' stage, the agreement is very imprecise and open to misinterpretation.

The employer is taking on an unspecified potential, the employee an indeterminate amount of work. Good interviewing practice, job descriptions, previous experience of the same type of work and the taking-up of references all create a more precise and mutual understanding.

A job description covers the work entailed, hours, shift times, payment, staff meals, behaviour and dress. But it can't describe what effort will be required. So it is a good idea to take on a willing applicant for a trial period before offering a permanent job.

> *If at interview stage prospective staff ask how much they will get paid and how much time off they will get, without asking pertinent questions about the restaurant and the job, then it's hardly worth continuing the dialogue.*

If taking on new chefs, ask them to cook a dish or two from your menu, then sit down with them and, over the tasting, discuss with them the outcome and what they would be able to contribute to the menu and style of cooking.

Although this may seem like a lengthy process, at least you will be able to choose a good chef rather than one who may look good on paper, but can't cook the simplest of dishes. And it will save you time and money in the long run.

> *Marco Pierre White, Britain's youngest three Michelin star chef and now restaurant owner, asks chefs to do the simplest of dishes – scrambled eggs.*

> *If any milk goes into the process and if no cream is added after the cooking, they have failed at the first hurdle. Simple, but effective, and it's quick and easy.*

During this process, you will be able to find out if the chef is familiar with, and knows how, to cook the ingredients on your menu. If the chef is unable to rise to the challenge of cooking steamed sea bass with a fennel sauce, for example, or even the best omelette, then you may not be talking the same culinary language.

To save time and money, find out as much as possible over the phone or by other means of communication before agreeing to an interview – and the cook-off.

> *Don't take advantage during an interview of asking the interviewee to work a whole shift. If you know what you're looking for, you will be able to tell within an hour of watching them work if they are the right person for the vacancy you wish to fill.*

Culinary checklist

You may also wish to have a culinary checklist to ask prospective staff about. Some possible subjects for the checklist:

What can you cook?

Pâtés and terrines	❑
Soups	❑
Breads	❑
Canapés	❑
Ice creams	❑
Sauces	❑
Dressings	❑
Game	❑
Fish	❑
Egg dishes: omelettes, eggs Benedict	❑

What can you do?

Butchery ❏

Larder experience ❏

Working out GP – the kitchen's gross profits ❏

Menu costing ❏

Purchasing ❏

Don't underestimate the applicant who applies for a job without qualifications and experience. If the person displays a real enthusiasm for, and knowledge of, food and has a passion for cooking and learning, they may be just the one to take on for a trial period. He or she may just have that creative side that those with certificates lack.

Interview objectives:

◆ To decide if the applicant is suitable for the job or how suitable the job is for the applicant.

◆ To decide if the applicant will fit into the existing team and into the organisation.

◆ To get across the essential expectations and requirements of the job. The interview can be seen as part of the induction process.

◆ To gather information, evaluate it and make a judgement.

◆ To find out about the applicant's skills, experience and character.

◆ To assess the interest of the applicant in your business.

Ask open questions, not ones that can only yield a yes or no answer:

◆ Tell me about your present job.

◆ What do you enjoy most about your job?

◆ Can you give me some examples?

◆ What did you enjoy about college?

◆ What did you get out of it?

◆ What made you decide to apply for the job?

◆ How do you find dealing with staff?

◆ Have you ever dealt with an uncooperative employee? What was the outcome?

◆ How do you feel about moving to this part of the country?

◆ How will this affect your home life?

When interviewing staff for either kitchen or front of house ask for references and follow them up.

During the interview

This applies to both kitchen and front of house staff. Do get across to potential staff the kind of high standards you expect from them especially in relation to:

◆ dress;

◆ cleanliness (are those nails and shoes clean?);

◆ behaviour (fag breaks are few and far between, for example, and not within eyesight of customers);

◆ flexibility (can they be called upon to do shifts at short notice?);

◆ attitude to customers;

◆ teamwork.

Find out if they are familiar with the type of food on offer and are willing to learn. Do they understand about wine and drinks service? If not, are they keen to find out? Can they work under pressure? With a smile? Are they motivated? Do they like working as part of a team? Do they look you in the eye?

You may sense that they are only working for the money and will be out of the door when the shift ends, not willing to add to the harmony and efficiency of the restaurant if extra tidying up or paperwork, for example, is required.

Do you, in turn, give the impression of good management and organisation? Do you offer a decent wage according to experience and skills? Do you come across as a caring person to whom staff can come in times of need? Are you approachable? Do you give enough information about your staff needs and expectations? Or will you impose on them, after they have started working for you, something that wasn't mentioned in interview? You should offer a clear, concise contract with hours, duties and pay structure.

If an employee is to respond to customers' needs they must know:

◆ what the product or service is; its full breadth and its limits;

◆ what the business can do and cannot do: false promises to staff can end in tears and recrimination;

◆ how to be sensitive and discreet about their place of employment.

Make sure you give this information to your employees and it is not found out by chance. Careful role definition and training is essential.

Other employment tips

Draw up a job description

No matter how simple or low-level the job, the more information you put down, the better your chances of getting the right person for the job. Cover areas such as skills needed, any training required and how much experience and responsibility the job demands.

Always take up references

Before someone joins your business, ensure you get references. For a fuller, more in-depth reply, phone the referee and ask questions such as 'Would you re-employ this person?'

Make your employees feel welcome

First impressions count, and the first three months of employment with a new boss and new colleagues is very important. Make your new employee feel welcome. Don't just pass them by and say 'Are you all right?', spend a few minutes with them to find out if they are feeling included, whether they are enjoying, or otherwise, the job, and so on. Give praise where it is due. Keep a list of birthdays and either wish staff a happy birthday or give them a card (if the business isn't too huge to handle this act of kindness).

A business is only as good as the people who work for it.

Involve your employees in the work culture from day one and keep them up to date with the progress of the restaurant and especially any potential future developments. Finding out from a third party can lead to disenchantment.

147

Appraise your staff regularly

Include a review system for each staff member. The business may have changed, perhaps creating more work for your staff and which they are finding difficult to absorb without a dip in quality and service. Discuss any issues with the full team present.

Enforce strict 'absence' procedures

In order to deal effectively with absenteeism and late arrival at work, staff should be very clear about company policy. A staff handbook is an ideal way to state policies clearly. To keep down costs, prepare it on an in-house computer rather than going to the expense of printing it.

Cover areas such as holidays, sickness, absenteeism, lateness, dress code, make-up, jewellery, hair colour, type of shoes, smoking policy and the use of mobile phones at work.

Casual labour

You may be short-staffed and take on friends, family or recruits from other sources at short notice. But set the boundaries even with them regarding the time required, payment per hour, breaks, cleanliness, jewellery, hair and dress code and whether they will receive a meal and free drinks, such as coffee and tea.

Overtime

If you need extra cover from existing staff you may make a couple of phone calls and arrange for some overtime. Simple. But overtime can run out of control. Firstly, it can undermine quality of service and secondly, it can undermine recruitment.

For example, people like to earn more, but tiredness can and does set in and good working practices can go by the board when staff are tired. What's more, the longer a vacancy exists for an extra staff member, the more existing staff get used to the extra money. When recruitment does take place and a new member joins the team, he or she may be resented as wages decrease for those who have become accustomed to the overtime.

Be aware and take action if a new member of staff is needed so that overtime doesn't spiral out of control. Its by-product will be a lowering of standards and creeping inefficiency.

Overtime and paying casual staff

If you are taking on casual staff, make sure you pay them at the end of their shift if this is all the time you have agreed to hire them for. Keep a record of any casual or overtime work so there are no disputes.

Agency staff will ask you to fill in a form to ensure you are happy with the work undertaken, agree to the hours to be paid and agree to extras such as transport, etc. The agency will send you an invoice.

Employers' responsibilities

When employing people for your new business the first thing to do is to call the New Employers' Helpline on 0845 60 70 143. The adviser will set up an employment record and send an Employer's Starter Pack with all information you need. Or you can arrange help from a business adviser from a local Business Support Team.

All services are free and you can also attend one of the local workshops on payroll. Phone them or visit www.inlandrevenue.gov.uk/bst/index.htm.

As an employer you are responsible for the following:

◆ Working out the tax and National Insurance contributions due each pay day.
◆ Keeping accurate and up-to-date records to back up any deduction in your accounts for wages, payments, benefits and the like relating to your employees.
◆ Making statutory sickness and maternity payments to your employees as appropriate.
◆ Making Student Loan deductions from an employee's earnings when directed to do so by the Inland Revenue.

◆ Paying Tax Credits to employees when so directed by the Inland Revenue.

◆ Paying deductions made over to the Inland Revenue Accounts Office each month – or quarterly if your average monthly payments are below £1,500 – after offsetting any tax credit payments.

◆ At the end of the tax year (April 5) telling the Inland Revenue how much each of your employees has earned and how much tax and NIC (National Insurance Contributions) deductions you have made. You must also give details of any expenses paid or benefits provided to your employees.

Useful telephone numbers and websites:

◆ Help with PAYE (Pay As You Earn) and/or NIC (National Insurance Contributions) for New Employers: 0845 607 0143.

◆ National Minimum Wage Helpline: 0845 600 0678.

◆ Employers' orderline for forms and stationery: 08457 646 646.

◆ Useful leaflets and pamphlets: www.inlandrevenue.gov.uk.

The law on pay and hours of work

Legislation is based on British labour law and European social policy for working hours and minimum pay levels, the focus being on:

◆ limiting working hours;

◆ protection from pressure to work excessive hours;

◆ guaranteed holiday pay;

◆ guaranteed rest periods;

◆ guaranteed minimum pay.

National minimum wage

The minimum wage is a legal right. The rates, effective as of October 1, 2007, are:

◆ £5.52 an hour for workers over 22 years old.

◆ £4.60 an hour for workers aged 18–21 and for workers aged 22 or over for six months after starting a new job with a new employer and receiving accredited training.

◆ £3.40 an hour for workers aged 16–17.

It is a criminal offence to refuse to pay the minimum wage with fines of up to £5,000. If you dismiss an employee when he or she becomes eligible for minimum wage payment, this is regarded as unfair dismissal.

Working time and pay regulations

An employer must not:

◆ require workers or employees to work more than an average of 48 hours a week, though workers and employees may choose to work longer;

◆ make unauthorised deductions from wages including complete non-payment.

An employer must:

◆ limit the normal working hours of night workers to an average of 8 hours in any 24-hour period. Although this doesn't affect restaurants presently as such, there may be restaurants in the future that open for 24 hours a day;

◆ provide daily, weekly and in-work rest, and four weeks' paid annual leave;

◆ provide all employees with an individual written pay statement at or before the time of payment. It must show gross pay and take-home pay with amounts and reasons for variable and fixed deductions. Alternatively, fixed deductions can be shown as a total sum, provided a written statement of these items is given in advance to each employee at least once a year.

Part-time workers' regulations

This is highly applicable to the restaurant business where many staff members are part-timers, and where the regulations are poorly adhered to. Part-time employees are not to be treated less favourably than full-time employees in relation to their contractual terms and conditions, pay equality, pension, annual holidays and training. For further information go to www.dti.gov.uk/er/ptime.htm.

Employing foreign nationals

Anyone you employ must be eligible to work and live in the UK. It is a criminal offence to employ any foreign national over 16 years of age who doesn't have the necessary permit. Currently, the maximum penalty is £5,000 per illegal employee.

Nationals of the following new member states of the European Economic Area (EEA) have been free to come to the UK to work from 1 May 2004: Poland, Lithuania, Estonia, Latvia, Slovenia, Slovakia, Hungary and the Czech Republic. Nationals who find a job and plan to work for more than one month, are required to register with the Home Office under the new Worker Registration Scheme as soon as they find work. Once they have been working legally in the UK for 12 months without a break, they will have full rights of free movement.

Those from Austria, Belgium, Cyprus, Italy, Liechtenstein, Denmark, Finland, France, Germany, Greece, Iceland, Ireland, Malta, Netherlands, Norway, Spain and Sweden have been able to work freely in the UK since membership of the EEA. Nationals from Cyprus and Malta have full free movement rights and are not required to obtain a workers registration certificate.

Many Australians, New Zealanders, Canadians and other Commonwealth nationals come to Britain to work with a good number of them working in the restaurant trade. Under the Working Holidaymakers Scheme, 17–30 year olds may work in Britain under this scheme for two years. They may work full or part-time and can apply once only, the stamp or endorsement clearly marked on their passport for the employer to check.

For a full list of Commonwealth members and for other information regarding employing foreign nationals, obtain comprehensive guidance for United Kingdom employers on changes in the law on preventing illegal working from www.ind.homeoffice.gov.uk. It can be downloaded. Or call the Employers' Helpline (0845 010 6677) for a booklet.

If you have employed a foreign national, the way to obtain a National Insurance number is for them to attend an 'evidence of identity' interview at the nearest job centre, taking with them their passport or proof of identity as well as evidence that they are working. For further details contact www.workingintheuk.gov.uk

Religious discrimination

The Equality Act 2006 makes it unlawful to discriminate on the grounds of religion or belief when providing goods and services. Since December 2003 it has been unlawful under the Employment Equality (Religion or Belief) Regulations to discriminate against a person on the grounds of their religion or belief in the area of employment and vocational training. For further information go to www.homeoffice.gov.uk, and visit the Equal Opportunities Commission's website: www.eoc.org.uk.

Maternity rights

Many stories are carried by the media on the flouting of the laws concerning pregnant employees. Avoid causing a legal hassle by following these points:

◆ Employers are required to protect the health and safety of employees who are pregnant, have recently given birth or are breast-feeding. These protections start as soon as the employee is pregnant.

◆ The contract of employment throughout the 18 weeks' ordinary maternity leave or any additional leave must be continued unless either party to the contract ends it or it expires.

◆ During maternity leave the employee should continue to receive all her contractual benefits, except wages.

◆ An employer must not dismiss an employee or select her for redundancy in preference to other comparable employees during her pregnancy or maternity leave just because she is pregnant.

◆ For further information: www.dti.gov.uk/employment/workandfamilies.

Paternity leave

Eligible employees can choose to take one week or two consecutive weeks' paternity leave, but not odd days. These usually need to be taken within 56 days of the child's birth. Legislation in this area is set to change as this book goes to press: see www.dti.gov.uk/employment/workandfamilies for up-to-date information.

153

Sick pay

Statutory Sick Pay is payable to workers who are unable to work due to sickness. Employers must pay sick pay up to a maximum of 28 weeks, but employees must satisfy the following conditions:

◆ over 16 and under 65;

◆ sick for at least four days in a row;

◆ earn, before tax and National Insurance, an average of £82 a week.

Employees are required to inform you as soon as possible that they are sick. They can obtain a sick note from their GP. For further information contact the Department of Trade and Industry: www.dti.gov.uk/employment.

Redundancy payment

An employer who makes an employee redundant is required to make a lump sum payment to the employee based on his or her age, length of service and rate of pay at the time of dismissal.

For further information contact 0870 1502 500 or the Department of Trade and Industry's website: www.dti.gov.uk/regs.

Stop and search of employees

You suspect one of your barmen of taking bottles of spirits home with him from the stockroom. There has also been a steady loss of expensive food from the kitchen and you think one of the kitchen staff is responsible. Just how entitled are you to search belongings for stolen property? If you detail a stop and search clause in the employees' contract, this will enable the employer to carry out a search and the employee must consent to the search. Employees may be disciplined or dismissed for a refusal to be searched as long as there is a clear, disciplinary policy in place.

Points to consider:

◆ Always seek consent from the employee before conducting a search.

◆ The employer could be charged with assault if the employee refuses to be searched, the search continuing regardless.

◆ Failure to ask for consent could result in a criminal prosecution and/or a claim of unfair dismissal.

Unfair dismissal

Employees who believe they have been unfairly dismissed can complain to an employment tribunal, generally subject to a qualifying period of one year's continuous service. Complaints can be made regardless of length of service if the dismissal is for certain specified reasons, e.g., pregnancy or maternity leave.

Trade union membership

All employees have a right to belong, or not belong, to a trade union. It is unlawful to refuse a person employment because he or she either is or is not a member of a trade union. It is also unlawful for employees to be dismissed or discriminated against because of their membership or non-membership of a trade union.

Equal pay

Employers must treat men and women equally on all counts including pay. If they are doing the same work or broadly similar work, they must be treated the same. Those who feel unfairly treated can go to an employment tribunal under the Equal Pay Act 1970 and claim up to 6 months' worth of payment. This includes pay arrears, sick pay, holiday pay, bonuses and overtime payments and can be claimed during a six year period (five in Scotland).

For more information contact www.tiger.gov.uk.

Age discrimination

Currently, of the estimated 1.6 million people employed in catering, nearly 36% are under 25. But the over 50s group are the most rapidly increasing sector in the labour force. As of October 1, 2006 it is unlawful for businesses to advertise for applicants who are 'aged between 20 and 35', for example, as this would treat those outside this age group less favourably and would be considered discriminatory. Equally, putting 'six or seven years' experience' in an advertisement means that it is unlikely that a 19-year-old would have the experience and is, therefore, seen as indirect discrimination. It would be difficult for the owners of the business to justify age discrimination unless they can show that there is a genuine business need.

Top tips:

◆ Avoid using words like 'young' or 'mature' in advertisements.

◆ Place advertisements in different publications to attract all age groups.

◆ Avoid age cut-offs for promotion.

Employment Equality (Age) Regulations came into force on October 1, 2006 and outlaw direct or indirect age discrimination in recruitment, employment and vocational training. As one third of the labour force will be over 50 by 2020, businesses increasingly need to recognise the benefits of age diversity.

Tipping

It isn't acceptable to put the customer on the spot when it comes to tipping. It is demeaning for staff and embarrassing for the customer. Adding a so-called 'discretionary' 10%, 12.5% (the norm) or especially a 15% service charge to the bill, forces the customer into a potentially uncomfortable position.

The industry would be better off without this custom and that of waiting staff asking if customers would like to leave a tip. Voluntary tipping shows appreciation of the professionalism of the staff and is seen by many customers as the best, most civilised option in the tipping game.

Of course, leaving a blank space in the bill which already has an added service charge is totally unacceptable and a sure way to kill off any repeat business.

Here's a novelty: pay your staff well so that they don't have to rely on tips to make a decent living.

The tronc

The tronc, a French word for alms box, is now the system of pooling tips. In the hospitality industry there is a tronc scheme.

An employer record with a tronc scheme type should be set up where:

◆ a separate, organised arrangement exists to distribute tips, gratitudes and/or service charges to employees;

◆ a troncmaster accepts and undertakes the duties of collection, custody and distribution of the tips.

Where employees retain cash tips handed to them directly by customers there are PAYE or NIC implications. The responsible PAYE office should seek to adjust the employees' PAYE code numbers where they are aware of these circumstances.

Does a tronc exist?

To enable you to accept that a tronc exists for tax purposes there must be evidence that there is an organised arrangement and a person who accepts that they are the troncmaster.

Ascertain the following:

◆ How monies are received by the tronc.

◆ Do employees pay cash tips in?

◆ Does the employer hand over tips, etc. included in cheque or card payments?

◆ Does the employer hand over service charges?

◆ Who keeps the monies before distribution?

◆ Where the money is kept.

◆ The basis of distribution and who decides it.

◆ How often the monies are shared.

◆ The extent of the principal employers' involvement, if any.

◆ Which staff are covered by the tronc.

◆ Whether the staff are aware of the tronc and the troncmaster.

◆ Whether the person identified as the troncmaster accepts and understands the position.

If there is any doubt about the existence of a tronc for tax purposes, you must accept that PAYE responsibility for tips remains with the employer for amounts which pass through their hands.

A tronc may still be valid for tax purposes even though:

◆ It only deals with tips and so on handed over by the employer which were amounts given as part of cheque or card payment.

◆ It only deals with any share of service charges handed to the tronc by the employer.

◆ The employer funds the tronc in whole or in part.

◆ The employer may have decided, or have been involved in setting up, the basis of distribution, but once the arrangement is set up the employer must not be involved in the process of distribution to tronc members.

Different occupational groups with the same principal employer may have different troncs (for example, a hotel may have one system for porters and another for restaurant staff).

Where the obligation lies with the employer to operate PAYE on tips, gratuities or service charges this obligation remains with the employer even if a tronc exists or the actual work of distributing the tips and so on is delegated to an employee.

For further information: www.hmrc.gov.uk.

Staff meals

One of the worst signals you can give your staff is to palm them off with a poor meal while on duty. What it says to them is that you don't place a value on them. How else will they learn about the food they are preparing and serving if they aren't offered it? They will have much more respect for you if given a meal that is both nourishing, delicious and shared by all at table before service.

Jill Dupleix, *The Times* newspaper cook and author, passed by London's *Kensington Place Restaurant* and spied staff sitting down to huge bowls of penne with meatballs and a green salad: this practice is good for building a team as well as helping staff to learn about the food served in the restaurant.

Another meal at *Zilli Fish* in Covent Garden was equally admired by Jill as staff ate a roasting tray of fat sardines sizzling in garlic and tomatoes, spaghetti with a chilli sauce and roasted red peppers and chicken thighs with a pizzaiola-style sauce.

Waiting staff eating some of the dishes on the menu will be better prepared to sell it, having also understood the process undergone by the cooking.

I passionately agree that restaurateurs should feed their staff well. It was one reason for my staff feeling included and well looked-after. I loved awakening them to different foods and styles of cooking. They were able to describe the food in more detail to customers who, in turn, felt confident about the ethos of the restaurant. However altruistic this may seem, it also helped staff to broaden their outlook and to feel part of a strong team.

Kitchen hierarchy

The professional kitchen's cooking staff are known as the brigade. Like many kitchen words, it comes from the French and, further back, *brigata*, from the Italian, a company or crew, its origins a military one. Look up the word in an Italian dictionary and you'll find it derives from the verb *brigare*, 'to brawl, wrangle or fight'.

The size of the brigade is dependent on the establishment, many small restaurants being based on a head chef, a sous chef and/or a commis chef, plus, perhaps, a kitchen porter whose job is primarily to wash up.

Or the staff may simply comprise the chef with waiting staff helping out with washing up and lesser preparations like plating desserts, prepping breads, butter and ancillaries.

Large restaurants will have an executive chef, head chef, senior and junior sous (under, literally: French) chefs, chefs de partie (those responsible for a section of the kitchen (sauces, larder, starters, mains, vegetables and desserts, for example), demi-chefs de partie (literally, half), commis (first and second) chef. Commis, a deputy or clerk, learns his or her trade from the bottom of the hierarchy. They are there to help, learn and watch.

There may also be a (rare) chef tournant, an all-purpose chef who is capable of all sections and who may be filling in for absent/holidaying chefs.

Definitions: from the lowest rank to the highest rank

Kitchen porter

Have respect for the KP, as they are affectionately known. Their job is an unenviable one of washing-up and who may also be offered the joys of prepping vegetables and washing salads. Be kind to the kitchen porter as he or she must endure repetitive tasks, the underpinning of the system.

The commis chef

OK, not the dream job envisaged by some, but this is the job to learn by. Duties may include plating up garnishes for all courses with some cooking involved plus, depending on the size of the restaurant, dealing with stock-taking and deliveries.

The demi chef de partie

This is the next step up: running a station with more responsibilities. It is time for the chef to prove him or herself and show a willingness to learn and work.

Chef de partie

Literally 'head of a team', the next quasi-military full rank up with the ability to organise other chefs. This is a managerial step up. In a small restaurant a chef de partie may be in charge of just one team whilst, in a large restaurant, he or she may be in charge of several teams. Duties could include staff meals, sauces, meat and fish prep and hot starters, for example.

Sous chef

This is the head chef's immediate number two and is capable of doing the head chef's job in his or her absence. In a larger kitchen there may be a junior or senior sous chef, in a smaller restaurant just the sous (under or sub) chef.

In a big kitchen, the sous chef essentially manages things, and does little cooking as a result of managing the kitchen, people, office work, rotas, food ordering, training: it is a position of authority. A junior sous chef is part chef, part manager.

Head chef

The head chef in any size kitchen is in charge. His or her only superior is the executive head chef who may be in charge of several restaurants, either independent ones or within a large company or establishment such as a hotel. In a small restaurant, the head chef is responsible for all cooking, ordering, management and training.

The head chef's jobs are to create menus, write the recipes or guidelines to go with the recipes, find the best suppliers, recruit, discipline and promote staff. In the absence of a sous chef, he or she is also responsible for rotas, giving out specific jobs such as larder work, cleaning, cooking, management and making sure the kitchen is up to scratch regarding hygiene and health inspections.

He or she is also responsible for reporting to overall management, discussing future strategies, special holiday catering such as Christmas, weddings and banqueting, dealing with customer and staff issues and stock-taking checks. Liaison with front of house staff may be delegated to the sous chef.

Women chefs

Who says they can't take the pace? There is this myth around – circulated by misogynists – that women aren't strong enough, can't stand the bad language and have an unfortunate attitude in the kitchen. They cry a lot, they can't lift heavy stock pots, they are moody because of their periods. They can't stand the pace and get flustered easily. Poppycock!

Women have a lot to prove – still – in this male-dominated trade. Many are perceived as being only good as pastry chefs, the discrimination still quite breathtaking. This is perhaps why I opened and ran a restaurant for eight years in Sussex as chef/owner, rather than work for unsympathetic, bullying characters. Of course it is a demanding job, but we women can hack it.

Witness head chefs Sally Clarke (*Clarke's*), Angela Hartnett (*The Connaught*), Ruth Rogers and Rose Gray (*River Café*), Samantha Clark (*Moro*), Helena Poulakka (*Sonny's*), all in London; Sonia Brooke-Little (*Churchill Arms*, Paxford, Gloucestershire) and Shirley Spear and Isobel Tomlin (*Three Chimneys*, Isle of Skye) representing some of the many excellent women head chefs in Britain.

Working together: kitchen and front of house staff relationships

Management is responsible for getting the relationship balance right, or, at least recognising the differing tensions within these two groups and settling any disputes and grievances that can build up.

The old adage of the customer is always right can be challenged here when it comes to food. When it is ready, it is at its peak condition and should be served immediately, not when the customer wishes to vacate the bar at his or her own convenience. This is where skilled waiting comes in, the waiter being the one who seats the customer and is aware of the order of priority the kitchen is working to.

For example, the waiter judges the timing for each table and reports back to the kitchen if diners are taking an inordinate amount of time over the first course. Or, conversely, if faster service is required.

A mutual respect must be built up between kitchen and front of house staff.

If the front of house staff don't understand kitchen staff's work pattern and degree of skill in putting each dish together then trust, confidence and the ability to communicate effectively breaks down.

This is where management comes in and should be aware of tension building up. Turn the tables and get them to perform each other's work or at least shadow different sections to understand their challenges and difficulties.

Staff behaviour

Your front of house staff and kitchen staff reflect the kind of restaurant you are running, therefore make sure of the following.

Appearance

If staff have a uniform, make sure it is clean, pressed, uniform in style and well-fitting.

If you operate a no-uniform policy, then stipulate what your staff should wear and be vigilant as to the features above. Do stipulate, too, the type of shoes, whether they are in good repair and are cleaned regularly, the wearing of jewellery, make-up and style of hair. Many restaurateurs demand that staff only wear wedding rings. They also oppose too much makeup and over-the-top hairstyles. This is a workplace, not a place for staff to be seen as partying.

Hygiene

All staff should have short, clean, unvarnished nails and must wash their hands after a fag break or going to the loo – or returning to duty after going to the shops, handling stock from a van, and so on.

All of the above applies, too, to kitchen staff: the cleanliness of their aprons, chef's jackets, the wearing of head gear are of paramount importance not only to the overall standards of hygiene, but also if seen by customers who will judge the restaurant accordingly.

No kitchen clothing such as chefs' jackets or aprons should be worn outside the premises as this could introduce dirt and germs on return into the kitchen.

Smoking

Smoking is a difficult subject in the restaurant business as there is a high ratio of smokers to non-smokers who simply can't live without a fag break.

◆ Be strict about these breaks as it is unfair on the non-smokers who have to pick up the slack.

◆ Make sure that smokers are not seen by customers hovering by an open door or by the bins as this really does give a poor impression.

◆ All smokers should wash their hands before service. If there is an all-pervading smell of smoking it can be a real turn-off for the customer (smoky clothes, breath, hands).

Banning smoking by staff can result in mutiny. You may be fortunate enough to employ non-smokers but, if not, be a vigilant manager/owner.

Drugs

Drug, alcohol and other substance abuse is everyone's concern. It damages health and causes absenteeism and reduced productivity. If you suspect any staff member has a drug problem, deal with it. If they come in late, don't turn up at all or show signs of drug and alcohol abuse, do you really want this kind of behaviour in your restaurant? No. A range of free leaflets providing advice and guidance is available from www.hse.gov.uk/alcoholdrugs:

◆ *Don't mix it – a guide for employers on alcohol*;

◆ *Drug misuse at work: a guide for employers*;

◆ *Passive smoking at work.*

Direct staff with such problems to helpful organisations including their own doctor's surgery.

To build your team rapport, finance outings and parties. Find out if your local gym and cinema can offer special discounts for your staff. Your staff will know by these acts that they are appreciated and valued.

Music

Music is often turned up for the benefit of staff who appear not to be able to live without it. Staff will also bring in their own type of music to inflict on the suffering public if management again isn't vigilant. Don't let this happen as it can spiral out of control and will soon be seen as a 'right'. See pages 53–5 for more information on music in your restaurant.

As a restaurant critic, I receive many letters from customers and the subject of music is one of the most frequent issues raised, apart from poor service and terrible food. If customers can't make themselves heard by other diners and staff, they will vote with their feet.

Service

Service is a mixed bag in Britain. Many waiting staff – and their employers who don't train them properly – don't see service as a profession but as a means to an end. Increasingly, however, foreign nationals are showing the British how it can, and should, be done. Some employers are taking the initiative and training their staff. This is not before time as the public's expectations have moved on from 'You alright there?' to a more acceptable professional way of service.

Dos and don'ts

Many of these points are basic common sense mixed with genuine hospitality. After all, you want these customers to come through your doors. You don't want to alienate them by showing indifference.

Meet customers at the door, if possible, and welcome them in. This is known as the 'magic minute,' It may not seem very long but customers can perceive it as longer if no one acknowledges their presence, and they may leave: there are plenty of other restaurants which welcome the business. Saying 'hello' to the customer in Britain often seems to be difficult. Other points:

◆ Do your staff speak English or the language of the restaurant? Can they communicate effectively without that language?

♦ Don't allow your staff to group by the bar, ignoring customers and carrying on a personal conversation.

♦ Do not allow staff to slam down the menu in front of the customer and ask in a bored voice what they would like even before they have had a look at the menu or board.

♦ Do make sure your staff look at customers in the eye, smile, offer a greeting, ask where they would like to sit (if this is an option), offer them a menu immediately and find out if they would like a drink immediately, or if they would prefer to wait until they have chosen from the menu.

♦ Do avoid the hard sell. Make your customers feel at ease.

Good service

Training your staff is essential. Get across to them your ethos, your expectations of what your gastropub or brasserie is all about.

Good waiting staff members are able to relate to each table's needs. Business tables, couples' tables and a family outing all need differing approaches.

Self respect and respect of others is paramount as is professionalism and efficiency. A good memory is also important.

Make sure waiting staff know what is on the menu and whether there are any specials which they can describe – but not in fast monotone. No one will be taking it in, with the result that the specials won't sell.

Waiting staff must not only be aware of what the dishes consist of, but also which wines are available by the glass, their types and what food they go with. They should also be knowledgeable about all the drinks on offer. What kind of coffee do you buy? What brandies are there?

Waiting staff should make sure that there is sufficient space on the table before serving. It's no good just pushing things around the table to fit them in as it creates tension with the customer and a feeling of not being looked after appropriately.

When it comes to the bill, be aware of people's needs. Watch their body language. Be prepared. Ask if they would like anything more. Be around. Don't buzz off to the kitchen to chat up the sous chef. Keep an unobtrusive eye on those valuable customers.

Lasting impressions: other service points

All staff should say goodbye to customers as warmly as they were greeted. This will create a lasting impression. People don't just go to restaurants for a good meal. They go for a good time out, a pleasing atmosphere and good service.

◆ Don't fawn. Don't ingratiate yourself. Don't be over-familiar.

◆ Don't be loud or noisy.

◆ Don't ever, ever be rude.

◆ Do be friendly, pleasant, efficient and professional.

◆ Enjoy yourself. But do keep your fingers off the volume control. It's not your party. It's theirs.

Top tips for professional waiting skills

◆ When seating three people at a table of four, for example, always remove the extra place setting. This applies to any table size when all seats aren't taken up.

◆ Hold the plate by placing four fingers under the plate and the thumb on the side, not on the surface, of the plate.

◆ Serve from the left and remove from the right.

◆ When holding two plates in one hand, balance one plate on the forearm by the wrist, the other underneath with three fingers under the second plate, thumb and small finger on the rim.

◆ Clear plates by balancing one plate as above for cutlery, the stronger part of the forearm and wrist bearing the weight of the cleared plates.

◆ Serve drinks from the right where the glass is positioned.

◆ To serve food without asking 'Who's having the pâté?' mentally identify each diner by number, starting, perhaps, with the one nearest to the bar as number one then going around clockwise.

◆ Orders must be written legibly, preferably in capitals, so that kitchen staff can readily identify each dish.

- Always add any other information (for example, 'medium-rare') clearly, the number of covers, the waiting staff member's name and table number.
- Always hold glasses by their stem, never the bowl.
- Clear the table after each course, leaving it set for the next course.
- Always make sure the table is left cleared ready for dessert or coffee with the removal of salt and pepper and unnecessary cutlery, for example.
- Clear plates only when everyone at a table has finished eating.

Management skills

A good manager shows self-confidence, has a complete understanding of the operation, maintains a good rapport between kitchen and restaurant and possesses charm. He or she is a leader, takes responsibility and can delegate well but must also be able to be hands-on without undermining other staff by, for example, showing them up in front of customers or other staff members.

The same dos and don'ts apply to the manager as to waiting staff.

The manager has ultimate control over the reservations and should plan the session successfully; they should delegate changes of seating to waiting staff to suit a particular party, special requirements and inform staff of such requirements.

The manager must be able to:

- Create the setting-up of a table plan of the restaurant and number each table. It is essential in either a large or small restaurant to achieve the maximum table take-up. This skill – taking up tables of four, two and other sizes – comes with practice.
- Create and implement a clear booking plan with space for name, number of covers, time, table number, contact telephone number and any special requirements or comments about the booking.
- Create a daily seating time-plan with times and numbers of customers.
- Liaise with the chef as to how many customers can be booked in at a time when the restaurant it at its most hectic. Or how many other tables can be accommodated if large parties are booked in. Balancing time and space is the key.

◆ Make sure that staff write in bookings in a legible way and that all staff know how to take bookings.

Staff rotas

Rotas are a vital tool to any restaurant so that, at a glance, everyone can see who is working or absent. They are made up on a weekly basis but, with good management, they can be worked out four weeks ahead of time, taking into consideration holidays, days off, staff shortages, overtime and busy times of year when more staff are required. Include managers in the rota to show that all staff are equal and accountable.

It is important to put your own or your chef's managerial skills into practice here and to be as fair to all staff members as far as possible. For example, unless specifically asked for, don't pile all the evening work on some staff members: give them equal numbers of day shifts as their co-workers so they have a night off with their family and friends.

> *Discuss the rota with all staff and follow up any complaints or dissatisfaction promptly, as grievances can build up.*

Include cleaning and refrigeration temperature-checking, too, on staff rotas so that they are brought to the forefront. They should be seen as a necessary part of the working week, not just something to be fitted in as and when, or done in a desultory fashion, or even forgotten.

Print out staff rotas and preferably reprint if there are a number of changes to a rota so that confusion doesn't arise resulting in a staff member not turning up, mistakenly thinking that he or she had swopped duties.

Below is an example of staff rotas for a small restaurant which is closed on Mondays, the sous chef taking over the chef's work on Thursdays and the roles reversed on Tuesdays. There may also be more part time waiting staff. If the owner is in charge of management he or she will be present most if not all days, but not necessarily all hours. Add these dates and times to the rota.

Staff	Tuesday	Wednesday	Thursday	Friday	Saturday	Sunday
Head Chef	8 – 2 pm 6 – 11 pm	10 – 2 pm 6 – 11 pm	Off	9 – 2 pm 6 – 11 pm	10 – 2 pm 6 – 11 pm	10 – 4 pm
Sous Chef	Off	10 – 2 pm 6 – 11 pm	9 – 2 pm 6 – 11 pm	10 – 2 pm 6 – 11 pm	10 – 2 pm 6 – 11 pm	10 – 4 pm
KP 1*	9 – 5 pm	5 – 11 pm	5 – 11 pm	9 – 5 pm	5 – 11 pm	Off
KP 2*	5 – 11 pm	Off	9 – 5 pm	5 – 11 pm	9 – 5 pm	9 – 5 pm
Waiter 1	Off	10 – 2 pm 6 – 11 pm	10 – 2 pm	6 – 11 pm	10 – 2 pm 6 – 11 pm	11 – 5 pm
Waiter 2	10 – 2 pm 6 – 11 pm	Off	6 – 11 pm	10 – 2 pm 6 – 11 pm	10 – 2 pm 6 – 11 pm	11 – 5 pm

* will also perform cleaning duties in the kitchen, restaurant, toilets.

Cleaning tips

Cleaning is an essential part of any food business necessary to minimise the risk of food contamination and infestation and to provide a pleasant and safe working environment.

To be effective, cleaning must be planned and incorporated into the staff rota:

◆ Adopt a clean as you go with spillages and food debris when preparing food.

◆ Draw up a list of all items of equipment and areas for cleaning and how often they need to be cleaned.

◆ Compile a separate list for toilet maintenance and cleaning.

◆ Specify what materials and equipment need to be used for equipment and specified areas.

◆ Also determine who is responsible for these jobs.

◆ Prepare a comprehensive, scheduled programme.

◆ Review the programme if there is a new piece of equipment or a new area.

◆ Store cleaning materials away from all food.

◆ Keep cleaning materials in their original containers.

◆ Don't mix cleaning materials, as noxious fumes can be given off.

◆ Never clean an area which is still being used by customers, with bleach or other strong-smelling cleaners, as the odour is extremely off-putting.

◆ If strong cleaning smells linger on after opening times, find another type of cleaning agent as customers really do dislike coming into a hospital-type smell and may not stay – or return.

◆ Wash hands after using any cleaning materials.

Choose your cleaning time appropriately: don't start washing down floors with strong disinfectant when customers are still at tables. This happened at one brasserie I was reviewing, the smell of the disinfectant literally killing off any desire to finish my meal – or to remain.

Sustainability

More and more pubs and restaurants are choosing to go down the sustainability route to help safeguard the world's resources and to address global warming issues.

You may decide:

◆ To have an Environmental Policy, and Health Safety and Community Policy, to share with all new staff when they join.

◆ To join the Green Tourism Business Scheme, which audits environmental performance and provides advice on further improvement.

◆ To use dimmer switches, sensor lights, low energy lights, and thermostats as much as possible, to cut down energy use.

◆ To buy equipment such as an efficient and environmentally-friendly washing-up machine.

◆ To buy cleaning products that are environmentally friendly.

◆ To buy Fair Trade sundries including water tumblers made from recycled glass.

◆ To use waste paper for notes and printing drafts and to use stationery and note pads made from recycled paper.

◆ To recycle all glass and cardboard.

◆ To buy half/full flush systems for toilets and waterless urinals.

◆ To buy local produce – if it is good, that is!

◆ To cut down on food air miles by not buying Kenyan green beans and South African cut flowers, for example.

◆ To find out more about where your produce comes from and if it is grown/reared ethically.

Useful websites

www.green-business.co.uk

www.towards-sustainability.co.uk

www.slowfood.com

11

Menus and suppliers

The importance of the menu: its selling points

The menu is one of three reasons why people come to your gastropub or brasserie, the others being the atmosphere and the service. But the food side of your business far outstrips the other two. If you don't have a good menu, a good chef and good produce, you might as well just open a bar.

Watch people reading a menu outside a restaurant and they will be weighing up the pros and cons of entering. They may have initially peered through the windows and taken into account the interior: the use of space, decor, staff, lighting and atmosphere. What determines their final decision? Your menu. Menus showcase the kitchen's abilities and strengths. They represent the coming together of restaurateur, chef, supplier and style of the restaurant.

Repeat-business customers know and trust your ethos, but those passers-by need to be seduced into coming in. The menu is a hugely important factor, not only because of its content, but also the way it is presented: clearly, concisely and in a readable font.

Gastropub and brasserie-style menus

As described in Chapter 1, gastropubs offer seasonal, fairly priced, unpretentious, home-cooked, mostly typical British food in informal surroundings. Brasseries offer the best in *la cuisine bourgeoise*. The hallmark of this cuisine is simple, classic dishes made from the best ingredients at an affordable price.

Both types of restaurants require the kitchen to source prime ingredients so that dishes can be quickly assembled or quickly cooked to order. The kitchen, of course, will make portions of *coq au vin* or *daube* and other slow-cooked dishes beforehand, and maybe offer them on a rotating basis during the week as specials.

The menu: food consistency

Your food has to be consistent. Of course the 'wow' factor is important, but the consistency of the food that emerges from the kitchen comes first. Your customers will desert you if the food on their plate doesn't match the last meal they had with you. If standards are allowed to slip, then you must re-examine your kitchen's strengths.

If you go down the more complex food route there is more of a chance that it will go wrong and you may not be a true brasserie or gastropub. If you change your chef, your replacement may not be able to rise to the challenge. You will risk losing your audience if his or her skills are not as great as the previous chef's, so chose your chefs carefully. See Chapter 10 on interviewing chefs.

Simplicity is the best way forward unless you have gifted, experienced chefs working for you. But even simplicity demands care and attention to detail. It is important that you and your chefs know which ingredients go together. Throwing a lot of good ingredients together without the knowledge of good food marriages will result in a unpleasant mishmash of tastes and ill-judged flavours.

The menu war of the sexes: Women start at the bottom of a menu and work up. They look for Death by Chocolate then justify the end of the meal by seeking out the most lettuce-rich dish at the beginning. Men start in the middle, where they look for the word 'sausage.' Once they've found that, they can safely locate something that is deep-fried and as far as possible, from the words 'goat's cheese'.

It takes three reads of a menu to get ordering right: the first to find the sausages; the second to see if there's an interesting alternative; and while your partner is ordering, that last, desperate scan to locate the sausages.

Never ask what's good: it's all good. And don't ask what they recommend. They'll recommend the leathery old monkfish that they've been trying to shift since Monday. Only have the monkfish if they recommend the sausages.

Guy Browning of The Guardian

Creating a menu

In order to create a menu, it is vital that your chef knows and understands the following:

◆ produce and combinations;
◆ how to cook them;
◆ the customer base.

The chef, Nico Ladenis, in his *My Gastronomy* cookbook, says that 'perfection is the result of simplicity. My philosophy is to be restrained in presentation, to produce each dish consistently and always approaching the ideal.' His own culinary marriages made in heaven include:

◆ duck and orange;
◆ salmon and sorrel;
◆ strawberries and cream;
◆ steak and chips;
◆ tomatoes and basil;
◆ chicken with tarragon;
◆ cold lobster with mayonnaise;
◆ lamb and garlic;
◆ fried eggs and bacon;
◆ *foie gras* and Sauternes;
◆ chicken and morels.

I would add steak with a Béarnaise sauce; fish soup with rouille, asparagus with Hollandaise sauce; salmon with a Beurre Blanc sauce; pork loin with crackling and real apple sauce; lamb with couscous; tiger prawns with Thai ingredients; caviar and chilled vodka; fish and chips; roast Mediterranean vegetables with goat's cheese; the best cheeses with appropriate bread and wine; bread and butter pudding made with brioche bread and a first class *crème anglaise*.

Nico's philosophy is to use the best ingredients. He questions a marriage between two meats, meat and shellfish or shellfish and fruit. Duck and lobster, duck and papaya, lobster and mango, beef with Cointreau and mango (seen on one menu recently), crab and beef are just some examples which do not sit comfortably together in a dish.

Good chefs know how to create a simple dish perfectly; how cook a steak or fish faultlessly; how to make a good vinaigrette and when to take the cheeses out to get them to room temperature, for example. Good chefs know how to time a dish, when to cook each dish to order and in what order.

Questions to ask when working out a menu

In the early days of putting a menu together, money and time can be wasted on some dishes. Questions that need answering include:

◆ Is it a worthwhile dish to develop?

◆ Are the ingredients available?

◆ What does my gross profit work out at for this dish?

◆ Does it keep well, or might there be high wastage?

◆ Does it present well?

◆ Can I delegate other chefs to do this dish in my absence, or are the skills not present in my current brigade?

If new to catering, you may wonder whether to change the whole menu at one go or introduce new dishes gradually. As a one-man band chef-restaurateur, I preferred to do the latter as to have changed everything at once would have created havoc, not only to the kitchen, but also to regular customers who like to see familiar dishes on the menu as well as being offered new ones. This reflects the vast majority of restaurateurs' and chefs' beliefs. Gastropub and brasserie menus tend to change at a slower pace. A core of regular dishes stay on the menu from day one, such as omelettes, ribeye steak and chips, plates of charcuterie and lemon tart in true gastropub/brasserie style.

Fine-tuning a dish takes a while. But if you are doing an assembly job – putting the best smoked salmon you can find, or oysters, or a fine ham with a chicory salad on the menu – then little fine tuning is required, the dish going on the menu right away.

When creating a new menu, do also look out for the number of hot and cold starters. If you put too many hot ones on, you will slow down the process of getting food out quickly to hungry, impatient customers. Getting that balance right is very important.

Garnishing your food

Be wary of over-elaboration. This can be seen by some chefs as adding a touch of sophistication to their dishes. Instead, it adds confusion and totally unnecessary clutter to the plate. What does a slice of orange have to do with a crispy duck and puy lentil salad or a fillet steak? Nothing. Food should look like food, particularly so in gastropubs and brasseries.

First-rate vs poor quality produce

If you source second-rate produce it won't taste any better if served on the finest china or the finest, whitest linen. It will simply smack of a case of the Emperor's Clothes. Nor will expensive carpets or décor help to disguise the fact that your restaurant is overcharging for poor food.

A good, honest restaurateur passionate about the business and customers will go out of his or her way to source the best produce around. This doesn't have to mean flying in duck from Paraguay or caviar from the Caspian.

What it means is:

◆ finding carrots that have flavour and cooking them with interest and knowledge;

◆ locating free range chickens that really taste like chicken and not blotting paper;

◆ tracking down very well-hung beef of note;

◆ buying good quality chocolate with high cocoa solids;

◆ finding a herb specialist who will supply French tarragon, not flavourless Russian tarragon;

◆ sourcing the basics with understanding and passion such as bread, butter, coffee and wine.

Good restaurateurs and chefs understand the way to perfection is via superb produce, the culinary job being simply to present these tracked-down flavours to the customer.

Don't go looking for difficulty. If certain produce is not available or is tricky to obtain on a regular basis, don't put that dish on the menu. Chefs must have peace of mind when ordering to fulfil a menu's promise. But don't compromise.

What to cook and why to cook it

Women chefs do tend to like cooking food they understand, their *raison d'etre* as a chef is often to give pleasure via the table. It is a huge buzz doing just this as I and many other women chefs can testify to. Many male chefs have the notion that they have to show off. Why? But before I alienate male readers, of course there are many male chefs who cook like their female counterparts, particularly those in gastropubs and brasseries as they are drawn to finding the best produce possible and cooking it simply.

Alice Waters, the remarkable and much-loved Californian restaurateur who started the trend of looking for the best produce cooked simply (and if she couldn't find she grew it) said: 'I opened a restaurant so that people could come and eat; remember that the final goal is to nourish and nurture those who gather at your table. It is there, within this nurturing process, that I have found the greatest satisfaction and sense of accomplishment.' It really is like that too.

Menu planning and dish creation

Planning the menu is an essential part of eating well. Professional chefs plan their menus with care, taking into account tastes, fashions, trends, health, seasonal food, limitations of time, budget and practicality. Choosing a wine list to go with your food is equally important. A balanced menu is a must.

When compiling ideas and seeking inspirational ideas for your menu, look firstly at what you wish to achieve, who you wish to attract to your restaurant and what the

178

kitchen can handle in terms of staff numbers. Consider, too, the ability of your chefs, your kitchen equipment and the cost involved in producing each dish.

Many chefs have a germ of an idea in mind when creating new dishes. Talk to people, read restaurant guide menus, research newspapers, cookbooks and magazines. You may also get inspiration from televison programmes. Going online and looking at gastropub and brasserie websites will also give you plenty of ideas.

It pays to think each idea through quite thoroughly before putting it on the menu. How much pre-prepping will this dish require? Can it be costed out favourably enough to put on the menu? Where do the ingredients come from? Does it fit in to the existing menu or does it upset the balance of fish, meat, vegetarian and sweet dishes?

Menu balance

Make sure you have a balanced menu to suit most people. Some tips:

◆ Be wary of putting too many cheese/fish/pork or chicken dishes instead of a balance of all of these.

◆ Don't put too many brown and beige dishes on the menu. You want to add colour to your food, not create bland-looking, unappetising food.

◆ Count up all the dairy produce or spicy dishes and trim them if there are too many.

◆ The same goes for a lot of fried food or carbohydrate-heavy dishes.

◆ Vegetarians don't appreciate several carbohydrate ingredients on the same plate, so balance it out with protein.

◆ Offer lighter meals as well as other dishes. These will be chosen by people in a hurry and those watching their weight.

Nico Ladenis himself didn't ask this question of balance often enough – one menu of his I recall demonstrating his fondness of offal with customers having to negotiate kidneys, liver, *foie gras* and sweetbreads with little else on offer. Sometimes even great chefs can get it wrong. Think of your customer, think of your own preferences and the kitchen's cooking skills and marry these three together.

Menu pricing

The aim of pricing is to achieve the best profits and ensuring the long-term success of the business. Ask yourself these questions:

◆ What type of customers am I looking to attract?

◆ What spend per head am I looking at?

◆ What quality of produce will I buy?

◆ What standards of cooking will be achieved?

◆ What is the standard of service and comfort in the restaurant?

◆ What is the competition like?

◆ What are the plans for the future?

You may wish to keep prices down initially to attract customers and become established. But the danger in this is that your loyal customers, when becoming aware of the price rises, may decamp elsewhere as they may not be able to afford you. Pricing is an area which needs flair, combined with a good business sense.

Restaurateurs on average should aim to have a 60–70% profit on food and a 60% profit on wines.

Create contented customers

Getting the temperature of the food right is crucial. Does the kitchen fiddle about trying to create a tower of jumbled ingredients, the food getting colder by the second? Or do they present the food quickly, dress it minimally (if at all)? Avoid having food returned because it is too cold. The kitchen will cook it again from scratch, thereby creating wastage and lowering your gross profit.

Customers want fast service, so get that wine, bread and water to them smartly. Their confidence in your business will soar.

A rule of thumb in busy gastropubs or brasseries is to get the first course out within ten minutes of the order being placed. Fifteen maximum. People may walk out if the half hour is breached. Keep the customer informed if there is a delay and offer them more bread or a free glass or wine. That is why it is so important to have a good selection of cold starters if the pace of your restaurant is fast.

Be aware, too, that there is nothing new under the sun when it comes to creating new dishes. It's just reinvention of the culinary wheel, but with top ingredients and good cooking, your food will stand out.

Taste what you put on the menu

Good chefs and restaurateurs always taste all their menu dishes. One young chef I interviewed for my chef's column informed me that he didn't need to taste the food he cooked as he had tasted it once and 'that was enough'. Hmmm. A good chef always tastes, tastes and tastes. The reason? Your salmon terrine might have a less strong tarragon added so it needs more, you may have not put enough lemon juice or salt and freshly ground pepper in. That ice cream needs more vanilla or coffee and the prawn and coconut dish could do with some more chilli. Could the rouille for the fish soup do with extra garlic?

Good food communication between kitchen and front of house

Good chefs always discuss each new dish with waiting staff so that they can talk to the customers with knowledge and be able to sell effectively. If staff just shrug their shoulders when a customer asks a question about a dish or say 'I'll just ask the chef what's in this dish', it will create a bad impression. There must be harmony and communication between cook and server.

The *Automobile Association Guide*'s ten top tips for better restaurant cooking

1. Source your suppliers carefully. Demand the best and only serve the best.
2. Use local produce where possible – if it's good enough.
3. Have one eye on the seasons –although most foods are available all year round, they nevertheless tend to be at their best for only one season.
4. Cook real food from whole raw ingredients.

5. Keep it simple, be true to the ingredients. Don't be creative just for the sake of it.

6. Always question – how can I improve this dish?

7. Taste the food you create. And remember the diner is eating more than just a forkful – so as a plateful, will it be too much, too heavy, too rich, or just plain boring?

8. Keep a sense of balance. Don't overcook, don't undercook, don't over-sauce, don't under-sauce, don't under-season. This sounds really basic, but it's where many meals fail.

9. Eat out. Get to know what the competition's doing.

10. Don't cook for accolades. The best food comes from a kitchen that has confidence in its own ability, where the chef is in tune with the needs of the restaurant's customer base.

Menu writing and compilation

Choose a font that is clear if you are printing the menus in-house. Be succinct and clear with your headings. State clearly any extras. Avoid too many supplements on a *table d'hôte* (set) menu. It might as well be an *à la carte* if there are too many. Tone down the descriptions. There is no need to add all the ingredients as this will confuse the reader.

On the next page is a sample past menu from *The Walnut Tree Inn*, Monmouthshire, Wales, which is succinct and clear, but the balance is somewhat questionable.

The balance is upset by pancetta in 2 of the 4 starters and with more pork in another starter. All four have a meat content. Breadcrumbs are found in two of the 8 dishes and more bread comes in the form of bread and butter pudding for dessert.

The majority of dishes are on the heavy, filling side, not in keeping with today's more light food. The ice creams will need explaining to each customer unless they are Italian-speaking. On the plus side, it does state the kitchen make its own food and sources local produce.

Walnut Tree Inn

Lunch menu

Two courses £16.95

Three courses £19.95

starters

leek and potato soup with pancetta

salad of endive, pancetta, shaved fennel, dolcelatte and rocket

home made terrine of wild Welsh rabbit with marrow chutney

crispy, breadcrumb belly pork with lemon, capers and fennel

main course

home made venison sausages with mash potatoes, greens and onion gravy

home made breadcrumbed fish cake with caesar salad

braised shoulder of local lamb with rosemary potatoes and greens

anna's lasagne bolognese

desserts

home made gelati and sorbetti

  gelati: gianduia, fior de latte, tutti frutti, stacciatella

  sorbetti: blackcurrant, wimberry, pear and saffron

vanilla pannacotta with bramley apple and raison compote & cinnamon crumble

panetonne bread and butter pudding

hot chocolate fondant with praline ice cream

Types of menus

There are two types of menu, the *table d'hôte* (table of the host), also known more familiarly as the set menu and the *à la carte* (from the card). The key difference between the two is that the *à la carte* has differently-priced dishes, the *table d'hôte* an inclusive price for the whole meal.

The *carte du jour* (literally, card of the day) is not very common these days and offers a fixed meal with one or more courses for a set price. A *prix fixe* (fixed price) menu is similar. Sometimes the price also includes a glass of wine or a substitute drink.

Brasseries often offer these set menus.

The *table d'hôte* menu (set menu):

◆ A menu with a fixed number of courses.

◆ Limited choice within each course.

◆ The price is fixed.

◆ The food is usually available at a set time.

The *à la carte* menu:

◆ The choice is larger than the *table d'hôte*.

◆ Each dish is priced separately.

◆ Each dish is generally cooked to order. Waiting time may be longer.

The advantages of the *table d'hôte* or set menu for the customer is that there are no hidden charges. The disadvantages are that the portions may be smaller and the customer has fewer choices.

The set menu's disadvantage is that the forecasting of how many dishes to prepare isn't straightforward. Too many dishes will lead to wastage. To get around this, keep the food as simple as possible.

For example, add a Roquefort and bacon salad to the starter list, rather than a salmon and avocado terrine, the latter more in keeping with an *à la carte* menu. The salad is easy and quick to prepare, the wastage minimal.

If you run out of prepared dishes on a set menu, be prepared to offer a more expensive dish with less profit. Therefore, keep the set menu simple, simple to prepare and inexpensive, so that all dishes can be quickly and effectively prepped to order.

Menu tips

◆ Choose ingredients seasonally.

◆ Choose lighter food for summer and more substantial food for winter, including fashionable, comfort food.

◆ Have a good balance of fish, meat, vegetables, cheeses and desserts.

◆ For example, have beef, lamb, chicken, offal, fish and vegetarian dishes, plus fruit-based, chocolate-based and cream-based desserts.

◆ Bear in mind that, as beef is expensive, this may end up as your loss-leader. You will have a better gross profit if staff can steer people towards other dishes.

◆ Include a selection of plainly-cooked food like grilled salmon, a light salad or be able to offer it should it be asked for.

◆ Have a balance of hot and cold food.

◆ Ask staff to steer customers towards more adventurous food on the menu. It may work in a smaller restaurant, although it may not practical in a large one.

◆ Change the menu, not only for the sake of the customer, but the chefs too. They mustn't get bored. This is when standards can slip.

◆ Remove dishes that don't sell to save wastage and your gross profit falling.

◆ Your specials board can reflect your buying prowess. If offered some good value, fresh fish by a trusted supplier on the day put it on the specials board, for example. It can also be helpful for chefs' creativity.

◆ Avoid putting food which is past sell-by-date on the specials board. Learn to plan ahead if some items aren't selling fast enough and then put them on the board. But don't jeopardise your business by trying to off-load going-off food. It's commercial suicide.

◆ Discuss the menu in detail with the kitchen staff and ask for their input.

◆ Don't even think about putting something on the menu just because it looks pretty. It has to taste pretty great too.

◆ Be wary of following fashions. You may end up with a mish-mash of dishes that the kitchen can't cope with.

◆ Be creative with the trimmings and leftovers. Will fish trimmings make a good fishcake for the specials board, for example? Will cheeses no longer fit to be seen on the cheese board be good for a specials board dish?

◆ You can afford to be ambiguous with something as specialised as game, as availability might suddenly dry up, substitution the only way forward: 'Game in season served in the traditional way, according to availability' might be an option to write on the menu.

◆ The advantage of having the menu written up (clearly) on a blackboard menu is that, if supplies run out of a certain vital ingredient like salmon, you wipe it off the board.

◆ Or if you write the menu on a daily basis if it's a small menu, just don't include the missing dish.

◆ If you're not making the profit margins, changes have to be made. Find out from another supplier their costs or determine whether you can find the same quality from another source by bypassing the middleman. Or take loss-making dishes off the menu altogether.

◆ One method that many chefs use is to add a £1 or so on to best-selling dishes. Your profits could be on track again.

Vegetarians

Increasing numbers of vegetarians appreciate dishes on menus specifically for them. These dishes are often the choice of meat eaters too, wishing to eat more lightly and healthily. You will find that if you take the effort to devise attractive alternatives to meat and fish, these dishes will be remarkably popular. And there is more to vegetarianism that pasta and omelettes. Seek out Mediterranean, Middle Eastern and Far East cookbooks for recipes for inspiration. Avoid gelatine and meat stocks.

Special diets

You will almost certainly have to deal with special diets for people with allergies, who are diabetic, those who wish for a low cholesterol diet or wish to follow a low salt regime.

Those with medical conditions or those who wish to follow strict eating guidelines will know what they can or can't eat. If the customer explains to a staff member that they are avoiding a particular ingredient they must find out from the chef if the diner's choice avoids these items. Guessing on the part of any staff member just won't do.

Allergies

Allergies can include the gluten in wheat, rye and barley. This allergy is known as coeliac. Other allergies can include peanuts and all derivatives, sesame seeds, cashews, pecans, brazil or walnuts as well as milk, fish, shellfish and eggs.

Diabetes

In those with diabetes, the body is unable to control the level of glucose within the blood. Diets may include avoiding high sugar dishes and some from the cholesterol list below.

Cholesterol

Those on low cholesterol diets avoid trans fats (found in processed foods like biscuits, margarine and pies) and limit amounts of animal fats. Preferred food includes lean meat, fish, fruit and vegetables, plus low fat milk, cheese and yoghurt.

Low salt (or sodium)

A reduction of salt in the cooking, or no salt at all.

Cultural and religious dietary restrictions

As our culture becomes more diverse, it may help to be aware of differing requirements by certain faiths and allowed methods of cooking.

Muslims

No meat, offal or animal fat unless it is halal meat (as required by Islamic dietary law).

Jews

No pork or pork products, no shellfish and no animal fats or gelatine from animals considered to be unclean or not slaughtered according to the prescribed manner. There are also restrictions on methods of preparation and cooking practices. The preparation and eating of meat and dairy produce at the same meal is not allowed.

Sikhs

No beef or pork and no halal meat. Sikhs may prefer a vegetarian diet.

187

Hindhus

No beef and rarely pork. Some Hindhus will not eat any other meats, fish or eggs.

Vegans

Vegans, although not in the religious category, also have specific diets and will not eat food of any animal origin. They will eat: vegetables, vegetable oils, cereals, fruits and seeds: tofu being an important staple dietary element. Any dish made with gelatine or stock made with beef, chicken or fish is not suitable for vegans. Be aware of what you add to vegan dishes to make sure you are abiding by their strict diet requirements.

Instructing kitchen staff

The head chef is responsible for teaching staff how to prepare special recipes. These recipes are a kind of shorthand, a checklist of ingredients and method with a variety of pointers, rather than the usual recipe found in cookbooks.

Develop a card system, or file away recipes on a computer so that you can always find the required recipe at short notice to give to a new chef who may not have cooked the dish before, or is not familiar with your method.

Compile a master file in which each recipe is kept under headings such as soups (hot and cold), salads (warm and cold), chicken, fish, beef, lamb, liver and so on.

For desserts you could have sub-headings such as ice creams, English puddings, fruit tarts, dairy desserts, pastries and basic preparations such as for proper custard and chocolate sauce.

Add the date when the dish was on the menu, where the original recipe came from and its page if from a cookbook. Cross-indexing is also helpful.

Add notes to recipes, too, if they have been modified. The oven temperature may need to be changed, for example.

> *For ease of teaching, stick to the metric or imperial system. This will simplify the work in the kitchen, everyone will be on the same wavelength (at least measurement-wise).*

Example of long recipe and its shortened version

Apple tart on puff pastry with a caramel sauce: for 2

4 Golden Delicious dessert apples, peeled, halved and cored
2 thin rounds of puff pastry 15 cm in diameter and pricked with a fork to prevent rising
10 g caster sugar
knob of butter
sugar syrup (see page 132)
caramel sauce (see page 134)

1. Pre-heat the oven to 170°C. Cut the apples into very thin slices and arrange around the pastry in a circle, starting at the edge and working towards the centre.
2. Sprinkle the apples with sugar then dot with the butter.
3. Place the tarts on a baking tray and bake for around 10–15 minutes or until the base is cooked and light brown. If the apples have not caramelised well, place under a grill or salamander, covering the edges of the pastry so that they don't burn. Or use a blow torch.
4. Glaze with the sugar syrup and serve with several tablespoonfuls of caramel sauce.

The reduced version:

Apple tart recipe: for 2

4 apples, peeled, cored and cut thinly
2 rounds of puff pastry
caster sugar
butter
sugar syrup (see recipe 210)
caramel sauce (see recipe 181)

Put apple slices on pastry in circles, sprinkle with sugar, add butter. Bake in 170°C oven until browned and caramelised. Continue with blow torch if necessary.
Glaze with sugar syrup. Garnish with caramel sauce.

Your key suppliers

A chef, no matter how brilliant, will not be able to metaphorically pull the rabbit from the hat if the produce they are cooking with is cheap and nasty. As food is increasingly simply prepared rather than more complicatedly cooked, the ingredients should be given centre stage. You won't be able to disguise a poorly-sourced chicken under a blanket of rich cream these days. Your food will be judged on its quality.

Therefore, choose your suppliers with the utmost care and work out your gross profit with quality at the forefront of all your calculations. Search for excellent meat, a good supplier of game and fish and top notch vegetables and fruit. Don't even think of skimping on quality cheeses, eggs, smoked foods, coffee and chocolate or even the salt and pepper you cook with and place on the table.

How to look for suppliers

Your bread is vital to get right. This sets the tone as this may be the first mouthful a customer has in your restaurant. Shop around for dried goods, olive oils and olives, or import directly some of these from a company abroad. Go to food fairs, events and local or regional exhibitions to track down the best produce.

Taste. Taste. Taste. If you have a good chutney at a restaurant, some excellent cheese or a smoked duck to die for, ask how to find these suppliers. Talk to other restaurateurs, the generous-hearted ones will be only too willing to pass on good suppliers to you and to tell you the ones to avoid.

Get price lists. Ask for samples. Bargain. Ask for wholesale prices. Consider buying by mail order. As a restaurant consultant employed to set up a restaurant kitchen, I go to as many exhibitions as possible to find the best quality food around. I take into account what the restaurant's aims are and its budget, as well as using other methods of sourcing.

Keep an eye out for produce in delicatessens and take down the company's name of products to sample. Consult the *Yellow Pages* for other sources, go on the web to locate cheese companies and other specialist companies. Cross the channel to buy more cheaply if you're in the south of England. But always think quality. Always ask to taste anything before buying. It's quite normal in France!

If you can, visit Borough Market, Borough Street, London, SE1 near London Bridge (0207 407 1002) for a short cut to finding superb produce.

Contact New Covent Garden Market in London and other major fruit and vegetable markets in your area for suppliers.

Once you have narrowed down your suppliers and started buying from them, always check your supplies and return anything that doesn't have quality stamped all over it.

Establish an excellent working rapport with your suppliers. This way they will look after you and will bend over backwards to keep your business. Always promptly query any accounting error and pay your bills on time.

You are not joined at the hip with your suppliers. Continue to locate even better ones.

Sourcing alternatives

The alternatives for local food sourcing are supermarkets, local wholesale and retail companies, cash and carry, specialist food companies, farmers' markets and getting your supplies directly from farmers and growers.

The choice is vast, the quality variable. Chefs often source their produce from a mix of the above, but remember to price produce diligently. Cash and carry companies aren't necessarily cheaper. Carry a notepad with the basics listed and do spot checks on prices.

Suppliers will usually call you to find out what your order is. Or call them. There is usually an after-hours ordering service to leave messages on for next day delivery.

Top tips:

◆ Fish is selling fast these days. Always, but always have the freshest fish. Once it's past its best, toss it. Or be prepared to lose a customer.

◆ Game is gaining momentum thanks to its healthy-eating tag. There is wild and farmed game and do try boar on your menu.

◆ Beef: demand longer hanging for your beef from your supplier: 28 days or more, nothing less. Look out for darker coloured, marbled meat.

◆ Vegetables: insist on the best for intense flavour. Go organic for tastier vegetables. Try different varieties. There's more to life than carrots.

◆ Fruit: it is worth doing some research to find really tasty fruit, apples in particular. Woolly peaches, dull apples and strawberries abound.

◆ Cheese: find a good cheese supplier – or three. Shop around for regional ones. Make sure your staff can identify the cheeses when serving them. Serve them at room temperature.

◆ Smoked salmon: there is some truly awful smoked salmon out there. Be discerning.

◆ Chocolate: don't just buy any chocolate. Source one with high cocoa solids.

◆ Coffee finishes off a good meal with character. Make sure yours is memorable. Source the best and invest in an espresso machine.

Kitchen supplies and suppliers

When I started as chef/restaurateur of *Soanes*, Petworth, West Sussex, in the 1980s, local produce-sourcing was impossible: the buying of excellent fish, vegetables and cheeses having to come from Covent Garden or Rungis, the Paris market.

Only the local butcher and a mushroom forager offered the goods I was seeking. I grew herbs and some vegetables and salads. Local wholesale suppliers could only offer second-class vegetables and fruit, dull, tasteless salads, even poorer tomatoes. The couldn't-care-less attitude was deeply dispiriting, hence the long-distance sourcing.

What it is possible to source

Today's restaurateurs are spoilt for choice if they wish to source quality produce. Local, regional and seasonal ingredients have the added advantage of helping to cut food miles and, as a result, pollution and fuel consumption. But do restaurateurs go down this route? The omens are increasingly promising as better restaurateurs offer locally- or regionally-sourced sausages, cheeses, meat, vegetables, fruit, wines, ciders and beers to their customers. They prefer to know the provenance of their supplies. But does the quality shine, the produce chosen with knowledge? Or is local and regional food buying merely paying lip service to trends? There is little point in buying local food if the quality isn't obvious.

Our tastebuds, having been assaulted by over-processed food over the years, could have become immune to quality. However, there is a growing band of chefs, restaurateurs and customers with heightened expectations and the standards of local and regional producers are improving. Customers relish the difference and celebrate the extra mile ironically travelled by the chef to source the best produce – and without stabilisers, additives and other 'benefits' of mass-produced food.

Multi-restaurant owner Sir Terence Conran says: 'I want to eat the cuisine of the country, democratic food. I am passionately interested in the improvement of quality ingredients cooked simply.'

Alice Waters, chef/owner of *Chez Panisse* in California, has, over three decades, developed a sixty-strong network of mostly local farmers and ranchers whose dedication to sustainable agriculture assures her restaurant of a steady supply of fresh, seasonal ingredients. This iconic chef, basing her commitment on French practices she witnessed on sabbatical in France after university, chose this non-compromising ethic right from the start: not to depend on unreliable quality and inconsistencies from commercial food wholesalers. Try to get a table at *Chez Panisse*.

Conran's and Waters' passion for this 'democratic' food is filtering through as a growing band of chefs and restaurateurs realise the untold benefits to their business of sourcing the best produce in the region.

Look at food on menus at restaurants listed in *The Good Food Guide* and other top guides and you will see an increase in provenance: Lincolnshire grey partridge, Goosenargh and Deben duck, Cumbrian fell-bred meat, Cotswolds, Nidderdale, Southdown, Wiltshire and organic Highgrove lamb, Dales-bred beef smoked and cured in Yorkshire ale. Rare-breed well-hung beef such as Longhorn rump, Black Welsh fillet from butchers are accredited by the Rare Breeds Survival Trust, the ingredients allowed to speak for themselves with minimal cooking and a return to simplicity.

Fish too is much sought-after, mindful restaurateurs sourcing eco-friendly fish from Cornwall and Devon, Cromer crab and Skye scallops, local and regional cheeses increasingly a commodity on this carefully chosen route.

Weaver's Shed restaurant in West Yorkshire goes one step further to produce their own chickens, ducks, quails' eggs and vegetables. Co-chef, co-owner Stephen Jackson's father, a retired CEO of a major company, grows cavolo nero, kholrabi, leeks, salads, soft fruits and no fewer than 75 herbs and wild plants for the transformed woollen mill. The saving, Stephen reckons, is £200 a week off the supplier bill, 'a sensible way of progressing and cooking within the seasons'.

Lawrence Murphy, chef/owner of *Fat Olives* in Emsworth, Hampshire, a brasserie-style restaurant, 'gets local rabbit and game and two guys fish for sea bass in the Solent for us', the menu reflecting this enthusiastic, innovative chef's local food sourcing that includes all vegetables and fruit in season.

The Star Inn at Harome, North Yorkshire, is a showcase of English-sourced food with most dishes markedly quoting their provenance. Yoadwarth Mill salmon, Whitby crab, North Sea lobster, Pickering watercress, Sand Hutton asparagus, Ryedale lamb, local fallow deer and Yorkshire Blue cheese are just some of the goods sourced by chef Andrew Pern, winner of many accolades thanks to his diligence.

Andrew is in the Alice Waters mould, sourcing seasonal produce within his own village, the Dexters bred for the table in view of the restaurant. Gloucester Old Spots are being reared in a nearby orchard on apples and 'everybody takes pride in their produce'. The network includes honey and duck eggs also from Harome and olive oils from Carluccio's.

'We've set the benchmark in the area with healthy competition from other pubs and restaurants upping the game', Andrew says. 'It's in everyone's interests.' The facts speak for themselves: over 1,000 people eat here every week.

How not to source your food

There are many national wholesale suppliers like Brakes (formerly Brake Bros) whose lorries criss-cross Britain and France, their buying power and market dominance creating an astonishing £1.4 billion annual turnover.

According to Brakes, there is no need for chefs to do any cooking whatsoever if sourcing Brake products: Cocktail BBQ Chicken drumlettes, Brake Crinkle Cut fries and Peach & Champagne Tart all medal winners at the 2003 British Frozen Food Federation Annual Awards.

The major supplier of frozen, chilled and ambient foods to the trade including Wetherspoons across the UK, Brakes' corporate message is a chilling one. 'Consumer and market trends', 'product assessment', 'total solution provider', 'customer to really focus on ... developing their branded estate', 'cost controls', 'pouch, c-pet tray or multi-portion foil' packaging with nary a foray into selling food with passion or indeed a regional or local slant. Buy ready-made soups, *Boeuf Bourguionne* (sic), mashed potato or salmon mousse to free up the 'busy chef' for executive paperwork.

Brakes' recipes are all part of the service. Witness Baked Garlic Chicken and Pancake Tagliatelle, cited product numbers given: 'simply thaw one Chicken Supreme (3042) and smother in garlic and herb cream cheese. Wrap in two rashers of thawed Beechwood Smoked Back Bacon (2806) and pan fry in 5 g butter for seven minutes each side.' Then you're asked to toss in Chopped Garlic (4017), shredded French Butter Crepes (3160) and Mange Tout (4741) in some more butter. Sprinkle with Finely Chopped Parsley (4019). *Voila*! You are a chef! No need to get down and dirty by doing the leg work in good food sourcing or real cooking, let alone think.

3663 ('spells food on your keyboard') is another nation-wide wholesale company whose sales are over £1 billion a year. They offer frozen and chilled food delivered by 1.000 vehicles to over 50,000 customers in the catering trade including *Pret A Manger*. Their 600 strong *Smart Choice* range includes ready meals, sauces, soups, canned produce and ice creams. Sales are booming. Think of those food miles by both companies. Think of the quality.

Food for thought

The less we know of food either via family, home economics, school meals, eating meals in a social setting – where food comes from, how it is grown, reared and produced – the less good, well-sourced food will matter.

If this is the public mindset of the future, hard-working, caring, responsible restaurants may be fighting a losing battle to move sourcing to an altogether higher level of quality. Good produce and skilful cooking may mean little to the next generation of chefs – and customers.

Raymond Blanc, chef/owner of the *Manoir Aux Quat' Saisons*, Oxford, contributes 'that British chefs desperately need to sharpen up. They're not connected with their food.'

He adds: 'How can we encourage the UK to move from cheap food to "real food"? This applies to everyone's food, not just in the restaurant trade.'

195

The British Protected Food Names Scheme

The British Protected Food Names Scheme is a British version of the *appellation controlée* system that exists in France to safeguard their wines. It has been in operation for 11 years with Cornish clotted cream and Jersey Royal potatoes as prime examples. PFNS's *raison d'être* is to protect regional and traditional foods whose authenticity and origin can be guaranteed through independent inspection. www.regionalfoodand drink.co.uk

Sourcing food from Britain and abroad

There is no doubt that eating out is even more pleasurable knowing where the food on our plates comes from, be it regional or local or, indeed, whether the olive oil or balsamic vinegar has been derived with passion and erudition from abroad.

Obviously not all produce can come from this country, the best *foie gras*, black pudding, cured hams like Parma, specialist cheeses, pistachios, limes, lentils and most wines are just a trickle of global riches reaching our shores.

The Slow Food Movement

Carlo Petrini is president of *Slow Food*, the Italian association formed by him in 1986 to defend Italian regional foods. It is now an international movement with 80,000 members, Mr Petrini believing that 'a gastronome who isn't an environmentalist is a fool', adding that people must know where food comes from and how it's produced.

It protects traditional foods at risk of extinction in many countries and includes safeguarding breeds of animals, wines, pulses, vegetables, fruits, cheeses, cured meat and fish. See their website at: www.slowfood.com. There is an active SF Movement in Britain (www.slowfood.org.uk) based in Ludlow, Shropshire with branches throughout the UK.

Quality and provenance of produce

Do we care enough as consumers? We have a vested interest in helping beleaguered farmers who look for alternatives in keeping their farms afloat, their animals' welfare and the quality of all yields at the top of the agenda. But the produce has to stand out.

Polytunnels, those industrialised structural eyesores, now produce up to 80% of summer fruit; 5,000 acres alone of Herefordshire, Kent and Scotland are now pastures of plastic. The season has been extended by months thanks to this method of growing. Just down the road from me is Tangmere airfield, part of the Battle of Britain strategy and now one of Europe's largest pepper nurseries with over 50 acres of glasshouses on its 115 acres of land.

Salads, herbs, vegetables, flowers and ingredients more likely to have been flown in from other parts of the world are now grown in polytunnels, the defence by growers being that 'it is British, good for local economy and we should be proud' despite a desecration of the landscape. The growth of polytunnels is largely due to supermarkets which demand reliable, unblemished fruit and vegetables.

BBC television gardener, Monty Don, mounted a campaign with others against strawberries, 'tasteless junk fruit' grown in 250 acres of 'ugly polytunnels' near his Herefordshire home when the company, S & A Davies, began building an 18 acre labour camp of 300 mobile homes and amenity centre. And won.

He, I and countless others query the quality of produce grown in these polytunnels, the scarring of the landscape and the misuse of migrant workers. Chefs, restaurateurs and the public should demand food that tastes of something, rather than simply accepting the current British strawberry, for example, which is 'helped' along by 17 fungicides and 16 insecticides. We all need to keep the pressure on or vote with our feet for a greener, more sustainable, definitely tastier Britain.

Useful contacts

Government agencies are included in this list. There are plenty of other producers to discover. Consult the *Yellow Pages*, your local council and websites via Google or others.

Just one word of warning: just because it's local doesn't necessarily mean it's good. Be choosy! Locate the best produce possible and help raise standards.

National, government and regional agencies and organisations

National Association of Farmers' Markets: www.farmersmarkets.net

DEFRA (Department Environment, Food and Rural Affairs): 0207 238 6687

Department of Agriculture and Rural Development: (Northern Ireland): www.dardni.gov.uk

Buckinghamshire Food Group:www.buckscc.gov.uk

East Anglian Fine Foods: www.foodanddrinkforum.co.uk

East Midlands Fine Foods: www.eastmidlandsfinefood.co.uk

Food From Britain: www.foodfrombritain.com

Guild of Fine Food Retailers: wwwfinefoodworld.co.uk

Hampshire Fare: www.hampshirefare.co.uk

Heart of England Fine Foods: www.heff.co.uk

Henrietta Green's Food Lovers' Club: www.foodloversbritain.com

Highland & Islands Enterprise: www.scottishfoodanddrink.com

Kentish Fare: www.kentishfare.co.uk

Local producers: www.buylocalfood.co.uk

London Food Link: www.londonfoodlink.org

North West Fine Foods: www.nw-fine-foods.co.uk

Northumbria Larder: www.northumbria-larder.co.uk

Oxfordshire Food Group: www. westoxon.gov.uk

South East Food Group Partnership: www.buylocalfood.co.uk

A Taste of Sussex at Sussex Enterprise: www.sussexenterprise.co.uk

Taste of the West: www.tasteofthewest.co.uk

Scottish Enterprise: www.scottishfoodanddrink.com

Scottish Food and Drink: www.sfdf.org.uk

Scottish Organic Producers Association: www.sopa.org.uk

A Taste of Ulster: www.nifda.co.uk

Tastes of Anglia: www.tastesofanglia.com

Wales: The True Taste: www.walesthetruetaste.com

Welsh Development Agency: www.foodwales.co.uk

Welsh Organic Meat: www.cambrianorganics.com

Yorkshire Regional Food Group: www.yorkshireregionalfoodgroup.co.uk

British Cheese Board: www.britishcheese.com

The British Herb Association: www.bhta.org.uk

British Sheep Dairying Association: www.sheepdairying.com

The Chocolate Society: www.chocolate.co.uk

The Cheese Web: www.gs.agvs.co.uk

Fairtrade Foundation: www.fairtrade.org.uk

Specialist Cheesemakers Association: www.specialistcheesemakers.co.uk

12

Stocking your bar:
wine, beers and other drinks

Gastropubs and brasseries have similar types of drinks with wines and beers leading the way. Gastropubs generally have small wine lists with limited wines by the glass, brasseries larger lists with plenty of choice by the glass.

Depending on the type and location of your gastropub, you may have a bigger selection of beers for the drinking-only bar trade as well as beers to match food. Both of these points are also applicable to brasseries, the original description of a brasserie being that of a restaurant that sells alcohol, especially beer.

Wine is one of the more misunderstood subjects for the would-be restaurateur: what to buy? How to buy and price it? How to sell it?

This chapter deals with:

◆ Wines.
◆ Wine buying.
◆ Storage.
◆ Guidance for compiling a wine list.
◆ Serving wine.
◆ How to deal with corked bottles.
◆ Wine and food and types of wine with food.

Wine diversity, a global market of wines from across the world, is also discussed and there is a helpful wine vocabulary list. Trading Standards guidelines for alcoholic weights and measurements are featured here too.

Beers can be divided into ales and lagers. Keg beer is filtered, pasteurised and chilled then packed into pressurised kegs while cask beer, or 'real ale', as it is often referred to, continues to ferment and mature in its cask or barrel.

I'll be covering beers more in depth also in this chapter such as traditional British styles, continental ones plus porter and stout as well as types of glasses and how to store beer. Beer with food will also be discussed.

Coffee, tea and water are also covered in this chapter, this trinity never more important to get right in this day and age.

Wines

The choice of wines is of paramount significance. Do you have enough storage space to be a serious contender for a good, lengthy wine list? Or you may only wish to have a small wine list instead, more suitable to a gastropub. Have you the knowledge to source wines to match your menu? It is vital to get wines right for your operation.

Tips for wine buying and storage

◆ First of all, sort out your storage. How much space do you have?

◆ Cellars are perfect for wine storage as they keep the wines at a constant cool temperature and the corks don't dry out.

◆ Wine doesn't like wildly fluctuating temperatures, vibration or warmth.

◆ Start with a small list as tying money up in wines can be costly.

◆ Seek the advice of a wine consultant or, perhaps, approach a wine writer if unsure yourself of how to put a list together.

◆ Wine consultants can provide a short cut to reputable suppliers who can supply wines on a consistent basis.

◆ Wine consultants and wine writers have a great knowledge of the trade and attend many wine tastings.

◆ They are generally freelance and are therefore subjective rather than tied to a particular supplier or producer.

◆ A good supplier will hold tastings for you and your staff and will keep cases in storage for you, the wines kept at the right temperature, too.

◆ A good supplier will go through the menu with you and marry wines to go with the food.

◆ The older wines get, the more carefully they need to be treated.

The diverse wine list

Gone are the days when French wine dominated the wine list. Wines from Australia, New Zealand, South Africa, Chile, Argentina, Spain, Italy and to a lesser extent, USA, Germany and Eastern Europe are chosen thanks to the growth of wine retailing. And, of course, the vast improvements in wine making. Canada's British Columbia wines are a case in point. Don't dismiss other countries' wines just because they may be unknown to you, the Lebanon, for example, having a long history in good wine-making. However, some brasseries do have a tendency to choose French wines if they wish to be seen as resolutely French in style.

Many wine lists go in search of wines to match the diversity of the global food that is now on our menus with the result that previously unknown grapes such as the spicy, fleshy Viognier, the musky, aromatic Pinot gris, the plummy voluptuous Merlot and the rich Shiraz are happily commonplace.

Go beyond the Chardonnays of this world. They have dominated the market for far too long and are seen as a desperately over-oaked cliché. There are, however, some better, unoaked ones from France, the New World ones having a tendency to be far more powerful and oaked.

Wine choices

◆ Choose good house wines, not poor quality ones.

◆ Not everyone likes Chardonnay, especially over-oaked ones.

◆ Choose several house wines of differing grapes: Sauvignon blanc, Semillon,

Chenin blanc, Viognier, Cabernet Sauvignon, Shiraz, Merlot, Tempranillo and Zinfandel just a few to choose from

◆ Most inexpensive and medium-priced wines are meant to be drunk immediately, i.e. not stored for future drinking.

◆ Have a good number of wines by the glass.

◆ Another popular way of selling wines is by the 50 centilitre or litre decanter and gives an extended feeling of informality.

◆ Have a wide-ranging list, not just the ones favoured by the restaurateur as it may not be broad enough for customers' own tastes.

◆ Avoid well-known supermarket wines. Customers know their price and may be appalled by the mark-up.

◆ Don't pawn the kitchen off with inferior wines to cook with. The poor quality will regrettably shine through.

◆ Heading of grape types with minimal information on the list is a help for customers who may not understand the differing grape tastes.

◆ The cooler the climate, the leaner the wine. The alcohol percentage can be as low as 9–11%.

◆ In hotter climates, wines will have tropical fruit flavours, many having a robust 14%–14.5% and even a syrupy 15% alcohol.

◆ Promote these wines well with information on tables, by the bar, in the window menu site.

Wine storage temperatures:

Wine should be stored in dark, secure, ventilation-free area which can be locked.

Red wine should be stored at 14°C–16°C and white wine at 10°C –12°C.

Wine list wording

Keep it simple. Phrases and words like 'excellent length' and 'cigar box aromas' are best avoided for the average restaurant, the mention of vintages and *premiers crus* (first growths) equally an alienating minefield for those customers with a shaky knowledge of wines.

Make the wine list headings accessible ones, like 'wines under £12', 'wines under £20'. Or go for the 'light bodied', 'medium bodied' and 'full bodied' which gives the customer instant access. Your wine list could have headings like mellow, spicy, dry or sweet for even greater simplicity.

It helps sales considerably to keep not only the wording simple, but also the headings. Entice the reader with your descriptions if using them. Be concise and enthusiastic. Avoid pomposity.

Of course, wording such as 'aromas of blackberry fruit', 'oaky earthiness' and 'ripe cherry fruit' can all conjure up an instant picture, but be aware of going down the totally over-the-top descriptive route. It has two disadvantages: customer confusion and it may highlight a poor understanding of wine by the restaurateur which doesn't inspire confidence.

You might wish to enlist the help of a wine writer or supplier with the wording. But be as succinct if possible, particularly if the list is a long one.

There is no need to put the alcoholic content of each wine on the list, but it may be appreciated as it can give an indication to those who prefer a less robust wine – or vice versa.

Tips for serving wine

◆ Choose glasses that complement wine. Don't even think of serving wine, no matter how inexpensive the wine is in Paris goblets as you've barely tasted or smelled the wine before swallowing it.

◆ Choose instead a plain, clear glass with a generously-sized bowl that tapers slightly before the rim. The stem should be long enough so the glass is held by the stem, not the bowl as body warmth will heat up the wine.

◆ Clean glasses properly, making sure that there is no washing liquid residue on the rim as this will destroy the taste of any wine.

◆ Glasses need to be stored bowl up, not step up to stop trapping stale air.

◆ Chill white wines, but not too much as this can dull their aroma and flavour.

◆ Red wines can be over-warmed in a warm restaurant, so take care where you store them, i.e. not near radiators, in a hot kitchen, in the bar by the coffee machine or by bright lights, etc.

◆ There is no need to pull the cork on wines an hour ahead of drinking. The majority of wines these days don't really need opening up as in past times when reds were likely to be tough and tannic.

◆ Restaurateurs need to be able to talk with a degree of knowledge to customers about wine in general and their wine list.

◆ Staff should know about wine. Get them tasting. Make up notes for each wine to give to staff.

◆ When serving wine, staff should always present the bottle to the customer before opening it. If not, then if the wrong wine is opened, you will have made a loss if the customer decides not to have it.

◆ Train staff to open a bottle properly by cutting the foil and removing the cork and never ever trying to extract a stubborn cork by placing the bottle between the knees and yanking it out.

◆ Train staff, too, to pour wine only half to two-thirds full in the glass so that your customers can enjoy the aroma, leaving room to swirl the wine around the glass.

◆ Customers increasingly like to be in control of their wine, the constant topping up by waiting staff in order to sell more wine is not acceptable: it's a hard-sell tactic which is not appreciated, the customer not returning. This is especially the case in gastropubs and brasseries.

◆ Always store wines on their sides, never upright.

Corked and other undrinkable wine

◆ Corked wine: a musty, dank smell caused by cork contamination. Replace.

◆ White wine with a sherry smell and usually with a dark yellow colour has been oxidised (too much air via the cork).

◆ Bad egg or drain smell indicates too much sulphur in the wine.

◆ Thin, sharp wine may not be to everyone's taste but if it's sour then it shouldn't be served.

◆ Stewed, baked, rather flabby red wine usually means over fermentation. Nor should this be served.

◆ Return all corked or tainted wine back to your suppliers.

Tips for selling wine

First of all, don't overcharge for wine. Your customers have chosen you for a more reasonable meal out and won't expect to pay upmarket restaurant prices. They will either choose the cheapest or, worse still, go elsewhere. Some tips:

◆ Promote wines of the month, for example, by the glass or bottle on a separate blackboard and make it legible.

◆ Promote seasonal wines, for example, easy summer whites or robust reds for fireside weather.

◆ Don't miss out on linking your food with a choice of wines.

◆ Organise wine tastings on quiet nights and get a wine merchant or wine writer in to discuss the wines.

◆ By choosing excellent glassware, you will encourage more wine sales.

Wine and food

Traditionally, white wine went with fish, red with meat. In Britain today, with its less strong food culture in contrast to Europe where food has changed little in comparison, we have borrowed extensively from the globe.

As a result, the guide book has been jettisoned. There are no hard and fast rules and no frankly dire combinations that will set the average teeth on edge. You may argue that plainly cooked fish isn't suited to a robust tannic red, but serve it with a fruity light red and it is a successful marriage.

Most meals benefit from having a lighter wine first then a fuller-bodied one, a drier wine before a sweeter one, a younger wine before a vintage one. Raw, steamed and poached food is more suited to a light wine, robust wines going better with roasts and chargrills.

Choosing wines to suit a whole table's customers, all of whom have chosen different dishes can prove problematic. A wine that will go with the majority is an answer, or choices by the glass for each individual may be the step to take.

Dessert wines are fast growing in popularity. Chill well and serve them in small glasses. Once opened, dessert wines will keep for longer than other wines. Look beyond the ubiquitous Muscat de Beaumes de Venise. The choice is sensational and dessert wines are good for profit margins. Add several types of dessert wines by the glass on your dessert menu.

Below is a general guide as to what type of wine suits what food but, as mentioned, the rules are here to be broken.

Whites and rosés

◆ Crisp, dry, fresh whites: salads, chicken and fish.

◆ Smooth, medium-bodied whites: pasta, creamy sauces, chicken, salmon.

◆ Full-bodied rich whites: lobster, turbot, slightly spicy style of Pacific Rim cooking.

◆ Aromatic and medium-dry whites: Riesling with spicy Thai food, Gewurtztraminer with Chinese, Tokay-Pinot Gris with *foie gras*.

◆ Rosé: making a comeback. Good with sharply dressed salads, summer food.

Reds

◆ Light, fruity reds: pasta, pizzas, chicken, vegetarian dishes.

◆ Smooth, medium-bodied reds: almost anything, French ones more suited to classic French dishes.

◆ Full-bodied reds: beef, game, casseroles and cold weather food. An enthusiast's wine.

Champagne and sparkling wines

They are surprisingly versatile. A richer, fuller-flavoured champagne can be drunk throughout a meal, but try demi-sec champagne with fruit-based desserts as dry champagne with a rich dessert doesn't work too well.

Dessert wines

These are pure nectar. Muscats and sweet Bordeaux go well with apple, pear, peach desserts. Australian liqueur Muscats partner chocolate with dash. Mavrodaphne of Patras, a red Greek dessert wine matches chocolate too.

> *People go first of all for the wine price, then the country of origin and then the grape.*

Pricing wine

Customers take issue with the high mark up of wines, especially if they recognise the wine that they can buy in a supermarket or a High Street wine merchant and know full well the retail cost. The next thought that occurs to customers is the wholesale price to the restaurant, i.e. the even lower price paid by the restaurateur and the resentment builds.

But, as Alistair Gibson, a wine merchant – rightly – states, retailers just have to buy in the wines and put them on the shelves. Their profit per bottle is around 28%.

A restaurateur, on the other hand, offers an experience, waiting staff, glasses, the cleaning of those glasses, a chair, table, perhaps music, all of which has to paid for on top of the rent, rates, insurance and all the other expenses that go with running a restaurant. There is also the money wrapped up in stock and keeping the wines in a good condition.

Therefore, a profit of 60% is the average for house wines, the other wines on that all-important list on a profit sliding scale. However, it is better to have those wines shifting than gathering dust, so offer a 'specials board' of wines by the glass or bottle.

Wine vocabulary

◆ *AOC*: *appellation d'origine controlée*, created by French authorities to establish specific areas of production, grape varieties and which also covers maximum yield per hectare, sugar and alcohol, pruning of the vine, cultivation and wine making methods.

◆ *Alcohol*: an essential element in wine, alcohol appears when enzymes created by yeasts change the sugar content of the grape juice into alcohol, carbon dioxide and heat.

◆ *Aroma*: the wine's scent defined by the type of grape(s), fermentation and the age of the wine. The bouquet.

◆ *Barrel fermented*: wine that is fermented in oak barrels rather than stainless steel tanks.

◆ *Blanc de Blancs*: literally 'white of whites', a white wine made with white grapes like a Champagne from Chardonnay grapes.

◆ *Blanc de Noirs*: white wine made from black grapes.

◆ *Blending*: also known as assemblage, is the mixing of types of wine varieties to make a more balanced wine. Bordeaux wines are usually a blend of Cabernet Sauvignon, Cabernet Franc and Merlot fermented grapes.

◆ *Body*: a wine with good tannic structure and good ageing potential.

◆ *Botrytis*: a mould that attacks grapes either as grey rot, which may endanger the harvest, or as noble rot, used to make luscious dessert wines such as Sauternes and the Hungarian Tokaji.

◆ *Claret*: the British name for Bordeaux red wines.

◆ *Cru*: literally, from French, a growth and dates back to 1855 to denote a vineyard's rank in Bordeaux which then divided into five classes or *crus*.

◆ *Cuvée*: literally, a vatful.

◆ *Decanting*: the separating of sediment of a wine, decanting from the bottle to a glass container adds more oxygen to the wine to make it more palatable. If the wine is old, it can be a disaster as it can cause a quicker deterioration.

◆ *Fermentation, alcoholic*: transformation of the sugar in the must into alcohol and carbon dioxide in the presence of yeast.

◆ *Fortified*: a wine which has had added wine spirit (brandy) like Port or Sherry.

◆ *Kabinett*: high-quality German wines.

◆ *Must*: unfermented grape juice obtained by crushing or pressing.

◆ *NV*: non-vintage.

◆ *Oxidised wine*: sherry-like or nutty flavour caused by the action of oxygen on wine due mainly to exposure to air, heat and light.

◆ *Reserve*: for special cuvées (vats) set aside for ageing or for future use. It also refers to a minimum ageing period for certain spirits like Calvados, Cognac or Armagnac.

◆ *Sec, secco, seco*: Dry in French, Italian and Portuguese or Spanish.

◆ *Spatlese*: late-harvested German wines.

◆ *Tannin*: different types of tannins created by the stalks, pips and skins from grapes plus nuts, wood bark and berries which are released during the fermentation process and the pressing. These tannins give the wine its specific character and contributes to its ageing. Wine storage in new wood allows extra tannins to be absorbed from the wood fibres to the wine.

◆ *Varietal*: a wine made from a single grape variety. In France the wine must contain 100% of the same variety but in other countries small proportions of other varieties may be added.

◆ *Vintage*: originally meaning the annual grape harvest, now meaning a wine from the harvest of a particular year. Each vintage depends on a combination of climatic factors which determine the wine's quality and potential for ageing.

Beers

There has been a remarkable change in where beer is sold in recent years with even the smartest of restaurants deciding to add beers to their drinks list. Witness, amongst others, London's Michelin-starred *Gavroche*'s beer list alongside its fabulous wine list. The reason? The rise of the gastropub is one reason, another is that brasseries have traditionally sold beer, and also more people are seeking out beers in less traditional surroundings. As more of us wish to eat out more casually, beer has finally come out from the cold and is being taken seriously. The rise of organic farming and local produce has seen a huge interest in local beers too.

Many notable gastropubs in the UK have remarkable beers. One, *The Drunken Duck* in the Lake District, started brewing its own beer in the cellars of the old inn and opened their own brewery, *Barngates Brewery*, as a result of its popularity. They now brew seven different types of ale and supply other pubs. Small independent breweries are increasing at a rate of 50–80 new businesses a year, thanks to our keenness to drink traditionally-crafted, local produce. Of course, gastropubs and brasseries can emulate *The Drunken Duck* in sourcing good local or regional beers without having to make them!

There are many types of beers with their own characteristics and qualities, changing consumer tastes affecting the sales of differing beers quite dramatically. Pubs, gastropubs and brasseries are beer's natural homes with many offering handpumped beers. Beer in pubs still accounts for three quarters of all drinks sales. Gastropubs and brasserie sales are on the increase as a result of the Real Ale campaign, locally brewed beers gaining in popularity and clever marketing by the large companies. Astonishingly, lager sales have increased by 49% since 1960.

> *Bitter is the most popular traditional beer in England and Wales.*

> *The final flavour of beer depends on all sorts of elements: from the variety of yeast to the minerals in the local water, not to mention storage in the pub.*

Beer styles

Beer can be fermented and brewed from rice, barley, corn, hops, water and yeast. It has been brewed for thousands of years, the Egyptians being the first known brewers. Today, thousands of different varieties of beer can be found throughout the world, but here are the types usually encountered in the UK and in Europe.

◆ *Ales* include bitter and mild, pale ale and brown ale. This group also includes India pale ale (IPA) and export ales. They range from mild and medium to strong and even sweet (Scottish export ale). The hop used can add a citrus or flowery bouquet and taste. Mild beer is often gentle, sweetish and generally lower in alcohol and often darker in colour.

◆ *Lagers* include German style pilsners with high hop bitterness and light colouring and European style pilsners with a medium body and low to medium hop bitterness and light colouring. American lager is light in body and colour with a clean, crisp, well carbonated style. Hop bitterness and aroma is negligible.

◆ *Porter* originated in London in 1730 and, although it has declined in popularity due to pale ales, it is gaining in interest. This medium- to full-bodied black beer has a hoppy bitterness and a slight malty sweetness.

◆ *Stout* is particularly popular in Ireland. The Irish-style type is black in colour with a distinctive dry-roasted bitterness and a medium body. The oatmeal stout is a medium to full-bodied beer with full chocolate/caramel flavour.

◆ *Ice beer* is brewed at colder than usual temperatures, then chilled to below freezing, creating crystals. These are filtered out leaving a smoother tasting beer with a slightly higher alcohol level.

◆ *Lambic beer* is brewed in Belgium with peaches, raspberries, cherries and wheat added during the brewing process. It is aged up to three years in wine barrels and when flavoured with the fruit and bottle matured, it becomes gueuze, a sweet, sharp, bubbly beer quite unlike anything in the British beer tradition.

◆ *Trappist beers*, also known as abbey beers, are brewed in Belgium and the Netherlands by Trappist monks. These rich, effervescent, complex beers contain high levels of alcohol and are usually dark in colour.

◆ *Bières de garde* from northern France and parts of Belgium (Wallonia) are sometimes sealed with a Champagne-wired cork. These amber or nut-brown beers are strong and characterful.

◆ *White beers* are gaining in popularity. These cloudy, light, refreshing beers go well with salads and light summer meals.

> *Two different types of yeast are added to beers: bottom and top.*
>
> *Bottom yeast settles at the bottom of the tank after converting all the sugar, the resulting beer is lager.*
>
> *Top yeast rises to the top of the tank when it's done with the sugar, the resulting beer is ale.*

Cider

Ciders are decidedly more popular these days thanks to a better made, less sweet product. Track down some local ones if possible.

Beer methods

Brewery-conditioned beers are ready to drink once they have left the brewery. They are sterilised. If being sold as draught beer it is put into kegs, sealed containers pressurised with gas. This beer is also sold in bottles or cans.

Cask-conditioned beers, also known as real ales or traditional beers, need time to condition in the cask. Cask beers may take around 48–72 hours before being ready to serve via a hand pump.

Dispensing beer is achieved by the handpull, a freeflow tap and metered dispense.

◆ Handpulls are the traditional way of serving cask-conditioned beer and are operated manually by pumping the handpull. This is not a suitable way of serving keg beer.

◆ Freeflow taps are used to raise the beer from kegs kept in the cellar. As this beer is kept under pressure the tap is manually held open to dispense the beer.

◆ Metered dispense is also used for keg beers. Metered units automatically dispense a half pint each time the switch is pressed. These must be calibrated and have a Government stamp, a Crown Stamp to confirm they have been approved by Trading Standards.

Breweries and pub companies offer cellar service to circumvent any problems with dispensing or cooling beer. Make sure you avail yourself of this service and have the numbers handy for emergency information and call-out.

Beer glassware

Good glassware plays an important part in the overall experience of beer. To enhance the taste, the smell and the visual impact, choose your beer glasses carefully. There is quite a minefield to cross when choosing your glassware due to stringent measurement laws and requirements.

Branded glassware, used to display drinks brands, is supplied free of charge by the drinks suppliers, or it can be bought at a discounted price. As they are seen as souvenirs, the loss rate can be high.

Legal draught beer and cider requirements

Although rarely seen, the third pint joins the half pint and pint glass in the size glass requirement. Draught beer and cider must be correctly measured using Government (Crown) stamped beer meters or Government (Crown) stamped glasses. There are three main categories of beer glass to be used in specific circumstances. Bear in mind that if using freeflow, handpull or metered forms of dispense, they all differ. The three sizes are:

◆ Unstamped, oversize glass.

◆ Government stamped lined glass.

◆ Government stamped brim glass.

Unstamped oversize glasses are legal only when using a Government stamped meter to dispense beer or lager.

Government stamped lined glasses are marked with a line to denote where the liquid part of the beer or cider should reach. These glasses are to be used with handpulls and freeflow forms of dispense.

Government stamped brim glasses will hold at least half a pint or a pint when filled to the brim. Allowing for the head on certain beers, the glass may not contain 100% liquid, therefore the customer can request a top-up. There can be a maximum of 5% head.

Cleaning your beer glasses

Make sure your glassware reflects your standards. Nothing spoils a glass of beer if it is served in a marked, scratched glass, or if it has lipstick or food attached to the rim. Any grease will make the beer go off as well as spoiling the taste. If using a glasswasher maintain and use it properly.

Use a clean cloth to wipe glasses. Make sure they are well rinsed so that no soap bubbles interfere with the taste of the beer. Don't store them rim down as this traps air. Hold glasses up to the light when polishing them to see all the marks to remove.

Throw out any chipped or marked glasses and replace them. It is a false economy to keep them as anyone who is offered such a glass will come to the conclusion this is not a well-run business.

Get cellar management training if you are selling cask beers in particular. All breweries and most pub companies run training courses.

Beer and food matches

With such a huge variety of beers – made with hops, malt, yeast and water – with extra ingredients including wheat, herbs, spices and fruit to choose from, it is no wonder that there is a minefield to cross when matching food and wine. CAMRA, the Campaign for Real Ale, has helpfully come up with the following:

Some suggested beer and food matches

Starters

  Soups

Vegetable	Pale bitters
Meaty	Malty ales
Shellfish	Stouts; porters; Belgian wheat beers
Fish	German lagers; light bitters; Belgian wheat beers
Pâté	Milds; Strong dark lagers
Quiches/soufflés	Light bitters

Main courses

Beef	Full-bodied bitters
Pork	Pilsners; Bavarian wheat beers; strong dark lagers
Lamb	Spicy malty ales; dark lagers
Chicken	Lagers; wheat beers
Turkey	Malty ales
Duck	Kriek
Game	Malty ales; Trappist ales
Sausages	Full-bodied bitters; dark lagers, Bavarian wheat beers
Meat pies	Full-bodied bitters
Barbecue	Smoked beers; dark lagers
Oriental	Wheat beers; ginger/spiced beers
Curries	Strong IPAs; premium lagers
Salads	Floral-hopped bitters; nutty, malty ales; wheat beers
Pizzas	Malty lagers
Ploughman's	Hoppy, fruity bitters

Cheeses

Mild	Light bitters
Stronger	Full-bodied ales
Mature / Blue	Trappist ales; old ales; barley wines

Desserts

Chocolate/Coffee	Porters; stouts; Belgian fruit beers
Red berry	Porters
Apple/Banana	Bavarian wheat beers
Creamy	Stouts
Spiced	Bavarian wheat beers

These guidelines have been taken from CAMRA's *Good Bottled Beer Guide* 4th Edition, by Jeff Evans.

Beautiful Beer is the beer and pub industry's campaign to revitalise the image of beer. It is led by the BBPA, the British Beer and Pub Association, with the support of its member brewers and pub companies and other industry bodies.

Beautiful Beer is the 'umbrella' brand for a number of activities, targeting the licensed trade and consumers, with the aim of encouraging more people to make beer their drink of choice on more occasions. Trade activity will focus on training licensees and their staff on beer standards and quality, as 'better beer makes better business'. See www.beerandpub.com, or call 020 7627 9191.

How to sell more beer

A few pointers to maximise your beer sales:

◆ Serve your beers at the correct temperature and in prime condition.

◆ Serve in sparkling clean glasses.

◆ Train your staff to pull pints properly and to be familiar with all beers, their styles and tastes.

◆ Make sure all your handpumps and other items on display are spotlessly clean.

◆ Offer customers a taste of different beers to help them make their choice.

◆ If you offer guest beers, make a feature of them, either on a blackboard or other signage.

◆ If you are using bottle fridges, make sure the customer can see the contents by good illumination. Keep them well stocked.

Useful websites

CAMRA (Campaign for Real Ale): www.camra.co.uk

Cask Marque: www.cask-marque.co.uk

Wine and Spirit Association: www.wsta.co.uk

Institute of Brewing and Distilling: www.ibd.org.uk

National Pub Watch: www.nationalpubwatch.org.uk

Other alcoholic drinks

Vodka and other colourless spirits have taken over the spirits market from whiskies, although gin is in decline too. Tequila, rum and bourbon sales are on the increase. People have turned to wines and beers – and water – as their preferred drink, spirit sales only accounting for around 5% of wet alcohol sales.

Some marketing tips:

◆ Stock major brands and group several types of whisky, brandy and others together to help the customer.

◆ Remove slow-moving brands.

◆ If selling by optics, have only 35 ml ones as 25 ml optics are seen as poor value.

◆ Place popular spirits by the till. This way they will be seen in this hot-spot.

Other drinks

You will, of course, be stocking your bar with soft drinks as well as all the mentioned alcoholic ones. Have the right type of glasses on adjacent shelving, also have to hand ice, lemon and other bar accoutrements such as corkscrews, wine coolers, ice buckets. Have available cleaning materials to keep the bar clean and tidy as well as clean tea towels for polishing glasses.

Trading Standards guidelines for selling alcohol

The pricing of all food and drink must be made clear to customers. Have a price list.

If you do chalk your food and drink up on boards, make sure they are easily seen and are legible.

What should be on the price list?

◆ The price.

◆ The quantity, for example, 25 ml of gin or half pint of beer.

◆ The price for each quantity. If the price of a double whisky isn't the same as two singles, then show both prices.

◆ Include VAT in the price.

Where should the price list be displayed?

This depends on the way the food and drink are served. Where customers pay for food and drink before consuming it – at the bar or elsewhere – you must display the priced list where food and drink are ordered.

If the price list can't be read from where the orders are taken, you should display a price list at the entrance to the eating area.

In restaurants, the price list should be displayed in the window or in the reception area so that customers can see prices before they enter the restaurant.

Obviously, this is not practical for most restaurants, these guidelines, perhaps, applying to vast chain bars and restaurants. A drinks list is the usual type of information given to the customer with the menu and this seems to suit establishments and trading standard officers alike.

However, weights and measures should be strictly adhered to. Despite Europe (which includes Britain of course) being metric, even Trading Standards are not going totally metric as you will note in the following:

◆ Beer, lager and cider, except when mixed with other drinks, can only be sold draught in these quantities:
third pint, half pint or multiples of half pint.

◆ Gin, whisky, rum and vodka: unless they are sold in cocktails, may only be sold
in these quantities:
25 ml, 35 ml or multiples of these quantities.

◆ Old imperial measures (gills) cannot be used for the sale of any spirits.

◆ A notice which is easy to read by customers must make it clear which quantity
applies: in quantities of 25 ml or multiples therof.

◆ The same quantity must apply in all the bars of pubs, restaurants or cafés.

◆ Optics or thimbles for measuring purposes must be stamped and where customers
can see them being used.

◆ If you run out of a particular drink, you must remove it from the price list as
soon as reasonably practicable.

◆ Wines must be sold in the following quantities:
  - by the bottle;
  - by the glass in 125 ml, 175 ml or multiples of these quantities;
  - these quantities must be made clear to customers either in a notice or on
    every wine list or menu;
  - by the carafe in 250 ml, 500 ml or 1 litre quantities.

This is not an authoritative interpretation of the law and is intended for guidance only
(courtesy of the West Sussex County Council). Contact your local council's Trading
Standards officers for further guidance.

Water, coffee and tea

Water, tea and coffee need to be looked at in depth as well as wine and beer.

Water

Water is almost automatically ordered these days with a huge upsurge in demand for
sparkling and still water. A remarkable two billion-plus bottles were bought in 2006,
the amount increasingly yearly.

With profit margins of 500% for most bottled water, some waiting staff, as directed by
their managers, are remarkably skilled at offering 'sparkling or still' as soon as the
customer is seated to reap maximum profit. What will you charge for water?

Although I am always for a fair profit, water pricing has, to my mind, become out of hand, many restaurateurs charging – wrongly, in my view – exorbitant amounts. This may be an attempt to grab back profits lost by wine and spirit drinkers cutting back. Or it may be sheer opportunism. I would urge restaurateurs to think again as it smacks of out and out greed and will be recognised as such.

A scam – yes, I see it as one – is to charge for filtered tap water, diners paying up to £4.50 for a litre which costs the princely sum of ten pence. I have also come across a scandalous £2.50 per glass.

Is this hospitality? No. But nor do you wish to be seen as a soft touch. Find your profits elsewhere or it could undermine customers' confidence in your restaurant.

Coffee

Coffee is so important for your restaurant. In previous chapters I have urged the necessity of either hiring or buying a good espresso machine to offer espresso, cappuccino, latte, americano and all the other coffees ending in '-ino'.

Gastropubs and brasseries are both seen as places to enjoy an excellent cup of coffee and to visit at different times of the day. Brasseries are, of course, the natural habitat of coffee drinkers at any time of the day.

People's expectations are such in today's restaurant market that good coffee is the norm either after a meal, with a meal, before a meal or instead of a meal. It is, to lovers of good coffee, the crowning glory to the end of a meal. Make it work for these aficionados in search of the best.

If you agree with my comments about water greed and the signals sent out by charging preposterous amounts, you will re-coup good profits by offering a prime commodity: fabulous coffee – but at a reasonable price.

But, in order to achieve this, the following points are best adhered to:

◆ Have an excellent coffee machine.
◆ Hire or buy it.
◆ Make doubly and trebly sure staff know how to operate it.

◆ Monitor your staff's ability to make excellent coffee and, if necessary, re-train them.

◆ The company you hire or buy your machine from will help you with this, but train all staff, new or old, well.

◆ Don't lock yourself into a long contract with a machine supplier.

◆ Experiment with coffee, sourcing good suppliers.

◆ Insist on a grinder for those wonderful beans you have so assiduously sourced.

◆ Have the right cups and saucers to show off your coffee. They may be sourced from the company that hires you the machine. Or buy appropriate cups and saucers. Dainty or 1970s squat, canteen-like cups are not suitable.

◆ If possible, go on coffee courses to understand the art of coffee.

◆ Market your coffee well.

Tea

Teas are on the increase in popularity. Do offer quality ones including peppermint and other flavoured teas. Don't charge overly for a teabag and some hot water if these hot drinks are offered after a meal. It could harm your business if you are seen as too greedy. But, of course, you must charge accordingly, the space taken up by customers – and time – must be taken into account.

13

The day-to-day running
of your restaurant

You've achieved your goal of opening a gastropub or brasserie and it's time to welcome in the paying public. You've put all that hard work into locating good premises; you've sorted out the finances, the Environmental Health Officer and other legalities. The furnishings and fixtures look just as you had hoped and planned and the kitchen is now fully stocked.

Marketing has been worked at assiduously and you want to test it. You are staffed, you are about to have your opening party and the word is out on the street: you are open.

But first, what is the day-to-day running of the restaurant like? Some front of house essentials and a day in the life of a small business kitchen is outlined, which may help to set you on course.

For every restaurant there is a pattern. No matter how many hours you are open, you must, on a day-to-day basis, deal with preparation, serving, clearing away and paperwork. Most restaurants start work from one to four hours before service depending on the type of food and service offered.

A well-run restaurant thinks ahead with its planning. If it doesn't it will be chaotic and the business will suffer.

In the morning, first-thing, a well-run kitchen's chefs will check the stocks (if they haven't done so the night before) making sure the menu's offerings can be adequately covered. Then ordering takes place of perishable goods, dry goods are also checked and ordered if necessary.

A restaurant that serves only food freshly cooked to order can prepare certain dishes to a point. This is called the *mise en place* (literally, the putting into place) – preparing all the raw material as far as possible, the assembly taking place when the order is received.

These preparations include soups, stocks, sauces, terrines, pâtés, boning and trimming meat and fish into portions and, increasingly in the gastropub and brasserie market, stews and *daubes* made with rabbit, chicken, beef, lamb and vegetarian ingredients. These form the bulk of the morning's preparation.

Vegetables, garnishes and other smaller kitchen tasks follow as well as a break and a staff meal before the restaurant is open.

All of this preparation is for speed of food delivery. Don't underestimate the amount of time it takes! Or if it takes too much time, consider revising your menu to suit your time, skills and staff's abilities.

In small kitchens there may be only one chef or a chef and commis chef. In larger ones the kitchen is divided into parties or sections for each section of the menu which may include starters, sauces, meats, fish, grills, vegetables, salads, larder and desserts.

Each section, when orders come through, will prepare its part, the final assembling of the food perhaps done by the head chef who will always check it before it leaves the kitchen. This is called the pass. The order will also have its final check to see if it matches before being taken to the table by waiting staff.

This is where the head chef shines. Can he or she generate the energy, help to create a vital teamwork and keep everything running smoothly?

When the last orders begin to trickle through this is the time when the clearing up begins in earnest although keeping a tidy, hygienic, clean kitchen during service is absolutely vital. Items not used are labelled and stored away or thrown out. There is no sense in keeping wilted rocket or parsley, for example.

If running an all day and evening food service restaurant, the menu will be a simpler one, but all the steps – cleanliness, clearing up, keeping a tidy kitchen, keeping a watch on perishables – must be adhered to.

Once the kitchen is back to its pristine state, staff can be released for a break before the next session. Or management might release staff gradually, the first one to leave being the first one back on duty to start the evening's preparation.

Front of house

Taking bookings: first impressions count

Your bookings book is by the phone on the bar or at some accessible place in the restaurant. Each day should have a separate bookings sheet or date. Have a plan of the restaurant at the front of the book so that staff can identify table numbers. In restaurant-speak, customers are referred to as 'covers.' Ensure that there is enough space in the bookings book for the following:

◆ Time of booking.

◆ Number of people booked in.

◆ Table booked (if applicable) – a window table may be asked for.

◆ Contact telephone number (if people ask why, it is for several reasons: if a booking needs to be changed or cancelled for any reason and, if a no-show or late, to be able to contact them).

◆ Any requests (disabled/special diet/birthday surprise cake and champagne).

A good restaurant staggers the bookings for the sake of the kitchen and the smooth running of the restaurant. But there will always be people who turn up late for their bookings who have neither contacted you or have not been contactable by you.

This can create a log-jam and they may have to wait in the bar, should you have one, until a table becomes available. Explain with tact. Offer them a menu, a drink (but not on the house unless the booking mistake was yours).

The booking sheet could also have the name of the staff member who took the booking if there are any queries.

Repeat back to the customer the booking to make doubly sure that the details are correct. Obviously, if a customer turns up and you have no record of the booking or it has been recorded on the wrong day with the wrong information ('I said a table for four, not two') you may have lost that customer forever.

Staff may be instructed to finish the conversation on the phone or if the booking has taken place in person by the customer with 'Thank you for your booking and we look forward to seeing you'. Little courtesies such as this one can only give confidence to the customer that this is a caring, polite restaurant.

A good manager and staff know how to fill a restaurant. They need to know whether table ten is going to be free in two hours and if people coming in are regulars and always like to sit at table ten. Regulars need that extra looking-after – and to be greeted by name.

Staff should also be aware of people with communication difficulties either when booking a table or taking an order. They should speak directly to the customer so that the face can be seen clearly. Speak normally but more distinctly. Listening attentively to all customers is 'A Good Thing'.

When customers come into the restaurant and if all staff are busy, the manager (if around) or another member of staff should at least smile a welcome and say 'I'll be right with you'. To ignore customers on entry will not win them over. They may feel unwelcome and leave.

When dealing with a customer, staff should make it a one-to-one transaction. It is very rude to ignore a customer or deal with them haphazardly or in a distracted way. Deal with one customer at a time. Give them your full attention and you will be appreciated.

Attention to detail is one of the most important issues to get right in the restaurant business.

Preparation of service

Your preparation may vary from a more formal restaurant if you have a more casual one, but many of the requirements remain the same. In other words, be prepared. This is the front of house *mise en place*, the preparation of service.

◆ Check the booking diary for reservations. Allocate tables to customers (if applicable). Check staff rota and staff present. Go over the menu with staff before and not during service. Waiting staff can make the difference between a good restaurant and a great one. Do they know what is in each dish and explain them to customers? Do staff look the part? Have they washed their hands before starting work? No excess jewellery or over-the-top hairstyles should be permitted.

◆ Make sure the menus are clean and complete. Discard any dirty or stained menus and wine/drinks lists. Has the specials board been agreed with the chef? Is it written up clearly? Are there any items not on the menu? Do all staff know what is 'off'?

◆ Is the bar area tidy and functional? Are the ice and lemons in place, white wine bottles replaced in the chiller? Red replaced in bins or racks? Is there a good stock of water, soft drinks and beer? Has the espresso/cappuccino machine been switched on and is it pristine?

◆ Check that the housekeeping been done satisfactorily such as sufficient loo paper, clean loos, empty bins, tables set properly, chairs wiped and dusted, any dead flowers thrown out and replaced by fresh ones.

◆ Salt and pepper containers need to be checked as well as cutlery drawer stock. Make sure too that there is enough change, enough pads to write orders on, the till has a roll in it and all the other little items that will help with the smooth running of your restaurant.

◆ The respect given to the manager/owner by the front of house staff should be the same as between kitchen staff and chefs. And the other way around. They are two teams working in parallel. There must be a good working relationship and good communication between these two groups of people.

Building up trust with your customers

Customers come in. Service has started. If the kitchen is behind with the orders, the chef must inform waiting staff so that they in turn can reassure the customer that they haven't been forgotten.

Ensure that waiting staff introduce each dish to the customer rather than just putting it down without so much as a glance. They are not going to be impressed. Explain what the dish is. 'Braised shoulder of lamb with rosemary potatoes and greens' is far better than 'lamb'. It's a courtesy thing.

If the tables are set up for four, two, six, eight or any number, and if all places are not taken, the entire setting or settings must be removed.

Rules of service haven't changed much over the decades with women being served first, all food served from the left and removed from the right. No plates are cleared until everyone has finished eating. Clearing away must be done with the minimum of fuss, clatter and skill. Once the main course has finished, salt, pepper, bread, butter must be cleared too. This is noted and appreciated by customers.

There will be always something to clear. Staff must be eagle-eyed and remove anything dirty to the kitchen or washing up area. While tidying up after a busy service, good staff keep an eye on the customers who may want another coffee, the bill or to ask a question.

Never be the kind of restaurant whose staff are so eager to sell another bottle of wine but are never around when the customer wants to pay the bill.

The manager must be aware of all tables. Is there one still waiting for a first course for half an hour? Deal with it calmly. A good manager is aware of who has been served, how long they have been waiting and if there is a problem that needs solving.

After lunchtime service, repeat the whole housekeeping, bar, menu, staff process over again including checking on the menu, the specials board and any changes for the next food service. Tables are laid for the next service, the bar re-stocked, menus checked for cleanliness.

Cash is counted and reconciled with the bill totals and another float added to the system. This is particularly important after every meal service and after every changeover of staff so that errors can be identified and discussed with the staff member in question.

If you are running a brasserie which serves food throughout the day, the process needs to be continually updated.

During a lull, it's time to keep up with the paperwork, the book-keeping, staff hours, invoices, letters of confirmation to a customer for a function and other necessities. Management and chefs may also be conducting staff interviews which should be put in the diary for either mid morning or mid afternoon. Or all of these may be taken over by management not involved in service.

Those new to the business may decide not take a break during sessions. It is very important to get some fresh air and a change of scene during that all-important lull between lunch and evening so do have a break then. This applies to all staff.

The kitchen

Depending on the size and nature of the restaurant, the start of the day differs. As chef/owner of a 28 cover restaurant I was responsible for the cooking, ordering, the *mise en place* and organising the staff. The restaurant was open from Tuesday lunch to Sunday lunch.

As someone once remarked, 'Sleep is like rat poison. After a while you get immune to it'. Yes, you do. But an afternoon cat nap can do wonders. Or that's what you do on your day off. If you don't have three children.

I started my day at 8.30 am, ready for service at noon. I was aided and abetted by two in the kitchen, Mrs O who did just about everything else, and Jenny who plated desserts and doubled up as a waitress. She was joined by other waiting staff on weekends and busy nights.

The menu changed seasonally, with a fish specials board. I started on prepping stocks, soups, pastry and terrines, the items that require longer cooking and prepping. My menu consisted usually of five starters, five mains and five desserts with an artisan cheese board.

It is essential to check the deliveries. Go through the order to see if it is complete and if the produce is of excellent quality. Return any produce that isn't acceptable with the van driver. Or if it's spotted later, call the supplier.

Start calling companies if deliveries are late (they could jeopardise lunch service) or if produce isn't up to scratch. As my restaurant was in a small town in the country, deliveries from London came twice weekly only, local produce daily if required.

Mid-morning: prep sauces, desserts and peripherals like dressings, making sure there is enough produce to cover an unexpectedly busy lunch period.

By late morning, lunchtime staff have arrived, the rolls are being baked, the butter put into dishes. Bookings are checked. All vegetables are now ready for both lunch and dinner service and are stored away. We all sit down to lunch and a briefing before service.

Service

Up the path come the first customers who are greeted in the conservatory and bar overlooking the South Downs. They may prefer a drink and to have their orders taken here or, if they are in a hurry, to go straight to the table and order.

Lunch is now in full swing, orders being put on pegs in strict rotation. Vegetables are being cooked to order in the Hobart steamer, the chargrill put to use for fish or calves' liver, a *beurre blanc* has its butter cubes whisked in, the salmon and tarragon terrine is being sliced and garnished, salads are dressed just before being served, a chocolate pithiviers has gone in the oven to be finished off and glazed then served with an almond sauce.

The swing door whisks open and shut between kitchen and restaurant. Laughter and the babble of voices come through to the kitchen where, surprisingly, there is little bumping into one another as we tend to anticipate our moves. Waiting staff wisely avoid getting near the stoves.

The cheeseboard is rescued from its chilly home (the law is an ass when it comes to being able to have cheeses at room temperature), five cheeses plated onto a rectangular dish with suitable breads and oat cakes in tow. The coffee machine hisses in the corner with yet another espresso emerging. Mine.

Service is over. The kitchen is left pristine. Staff leave for the afternoon, returning at

6 pm for a 7 pm start. Fridges are checked for produce and a list is made on the board of prepping to do.

At 6 pm rolls go in to be finished off, bookings are checked and the stock pots are strained, cleaned and put away to leave more room for a busy evening's cooking. Staff arrive, a meal is either eaten or, quite often, they eat off the menu after service at the high kitchen table to go through the day and discuss anything that went wrong – or right! Or discuss improvements that can be made, adjustments to the menu that might improve the sale of certain dishes and any feedback that emerges.

But, before this meal, it's showtime! The orders come in, the plated food goes out garnished and followed by suitable vegetables; desserts are plated and served. Chicken breasts spatter their skin fat on the range, steam rises from the mussels and the door between the pass flaps in and out.

That wonderful pressure is on to do 28 starters, main courses and desserts, the layering of the thought processes – which dish is cooked when – as complicated as attempting to play a game of tag with 28 people simultaneously.

Just two more orders to go: 'Please don't have the scallops with pea purée, I've only got one more portion!' They don't and go instead for roast sea bass with a sesame prawn crust, chargrilled lamb with a garlic sauce, wild mushroom risotto and beef fillet with Dauphinoise potatoes. Then suddenly the restaurant is empty, apart from regular customers chewing the fat with front of house. The kitchen is scrubbed down, rubbish is put out and staff check their rota after their meal.

It's nearly midnight. Staff rev up their cars or motor bikes in the car park and leave, the South Downs beyond lit up by a flash of lightning. It's beautiful. And quiet again. But there's still the ordering to do on the phone, some more checking of produce and then the kitchen lights go out for another day.

It's a buzz. Why do people do it? For that – and being creative, giving pleasure. It's about working, learning, growing as a team, trying out new ideas and meeting interesting people. It is mostly sheer fun. It's pure theatre. It's a living. And it sure beats working in an office.

Of course my own experiences are very different from those in a large kitchen or in another type of restaurant. Treble, quadruple the covers, the staff, the produce, the size of the organisation and it has to be even more scrupulously and meticulously worked out. It is essential to be disciplined for it to work properly. Some see it as organised chaos, some as a thing of beauty.

> *There are ordering sheets, stock sheets, staff personnel information, kitchen equipment maintenance sheets and records of fridge temperatures to check on a daily basis. Chefs have a notebook or computer records for recipes and ingredients and when certain dishes were put on the menu. The head chef's management skills must be on a par with cooking skills and menu development.*

14

Customer relations and being a customer

Running a restaurant is mainly about the responsibilities the restaurant has towards its customers and staff. But what are the responsibilities of the customer towards your gastropub or brasserie? This chapter outlines both of these obligations and, with a foot in both camps, putting yourself in your customers' shoes.

Handling customers is a skill that will come with the running of a restaurant. If you don't already possess the necessary skills it may be helpful to have some points laid out beforehand to help you on your way.

As hotelier and restaurateur Kit Chapman (*Castle Hotel* and *Brazz* chain), in his *An Innkeeper's Diary*, reports: 'Our clients are getting more demanding and difficult, not less. Attention to detail is the mantra we chant and success relies on our ability to respond to their wishes.'

'A carefully planned, well organised, perfectly well executed party is no guarantee of a satisfied customer. Any number of complex human ingredients may intervene: mood, prejudice, fear, personal taste, class snobbery, social inadequacy, megalomania, a row with the wife, the death of a pet. (Take your pick.) We're in the mind-game – party psychology, part clairvoyance. We're in the business of making magic.'

How true. And how succinctly put, if a trifle depressing. However, it does help to understand what the hospitality business is about and what it can achieve if taking on board the complex nature of people.

Recognising dissatisfied customers

Good management recognises the decline of customer satisfaction, the symptoms being:

◆ increasing complaints about the staff;

◆ increasing complaints about the food or produce;

◆ more accidents taking place in the restaurant due to poor maintenance;

◆ arguments between staff which affects the atmosphere;

◆ poor morale in the business;

◆ breakages or shortages of equipment resulting in staff being unable to do their job properly which, in turn, affects the customer;

◆ high turnover of staff.

Customers may also be aware of the lowering of standards by staff:

◆ Do they smile at customers? Or not?

◆ Are they courteous towards customers? Or not?

◆ Do they say 'please', 'thank you', 'excuse me'?

◆ Management might ask themselves if the staff member is in the right job or if there is a problem to be solved.

◆ Do they greet customers or congregate around the bar, ignoring them?

Handling complaints

If a problem arises and a customer makes a complaint, the following may be of help:

◆ don't interrupt the customer;

◆ never lose your temper;

◆ don't take it personally (hard, I know!);

◆ don't argue;

◆ don't place the blame on another person.

But:

◆ do apologise for the specific complaint;

◆ do move into a quieter area with the customer to discuss the complaint so as not to upset other customers;

◆ do re-state the complaint to show you understand the nature of the problem;

◆ do agree that the customer was right to bring that particular problem up;

◆ act in a quiet, professional manner;

◆ by keeping your voice low the customer's anger can partly be dispelled;

◆ if you feel their complaint was justified, then do offer to take the offending dish off the bill, if this was the problem and replace it if applicable;

◆ if it was the service, a glass of wine, a bottle, or free coffees all around might pacify dissatisfied customers. Don't expect them to pay the service charge.

Customer satisfaction

This summing-up list highlights factors which make up a good restaurant experience.

◆ The welcome, décor and ambience.

◆ The manner in which an enquiry or booking is taken.

◆ The location of the table.

◆ The menu and drinks list (contents and cleanliness of the lists).

◆ How the order is taken.

◆ Availability of the food on the menu.

◆ The speed and efficiency of service.

◆ How pleasant and courteous staff are.

◆ The staff's unobtrusive waiting skills and attentiveness.

◆ The ability to attract the attention of staff.

◆ Other customers' behaviour (rowdy, drunk, overuse of mobile phones, etc.)

◆ Method of handling complaints.

◆ Method of presenting the bill and collecting of the payment.

◆ The departure and how this is handled (ignoring departing customers, being off-hand or the opposite).

Putting yourself in your customers' shoes

Watch your staff to see if they welcome customers. If your staff are around the bar, talking to one another rather than keeping an eye on the customers, it's up to you to train them to understand what their job entails.

Sit at all of your tables during service and look around you. What do you observe?

1. Are the chairs comfortable? Suitable for the type of operation you run? If you are sitting for a length of time over a meal of merit you don't want to squirm uncomfortably in your seat.

2. Would you really want to sit next to a loo door? A swinging kitchen door with all the clatter of a busy kitchen? By a draught from the front door? By coat hangers, coats brushing against your chair and, maybe, you?

3. Are the tables big enough for placing bottles of wine, water, serving dishes, candles, flowers, cutlery, napkins and oversize plates? If not, what are you going to do about it?

4. Are the tables clean and wiped down properly before a customer sits at one?

5. Are the surroundings clean? Are those cobwebs and dirty marks on the ceilings, walls and skirting boards?

6. Why are these dirty and torn menus been given to customers?

7. Why are there streaks on the cutlery and glasses?

8. Why are these flowers past their sell-by date and not replaced?

9. Why is the bar looking as if a bomb has hit it?

10.Why haven't all those dirty glasses on the bar been moved to the washing up area and not left in full view of customers?

11.Have the staff washed their hands or is that a dirty thumbnail?

12.Are waiting staff, when serving the food, telling the customers what the dishes are in some detail and not just saying 'fish, pâté, soup, meat'?

13.Why are the tables not being cleared properly and quickly?

14.Why is a staff member's shirt hanging out and shoes are not cleaned and polished?

15.Why are the windows dirty or smudged?

You may also notice the following:

◆ What are staff doing hanging out by the bins in full view of customers and having a cigarette break?

◆ Why is the music so loud? Is this my restaurant's policy or are the staff upping the volume while I or the manager is away?

◆ Why are the toilets not cleaned and well stocked with toilet paper, soap and paper towels? Why has a rota system I put in place not worked? Or is there not one in place?

◆ Why are there grubby marks on doors to the toilets, the kitchen and the entrance doors?

You may also ask yourself these kitchen-based questions:

◆ Why is the kitchen in a mess? Why hasn't it been cleaned properly?

◆ Why is this food uncovered on a kitchen counter?

◆ Why are the bins overflowing?

◆ Why has this tired lettuce leaf been put on a plate as a garnish?

◆ Why am I eating a chicken breast that tastes of nothing, or is of poor quality? Is the chef not ordering well and with care? Is the cooking up to scratch?

◆ Why is this stale bread being served to customers?

◆ Why is the wine not being sufficiently chilled?

◆ Why does this dish look as if it's been thrown onto the plate rather than being prepared and plated with due care and attention?

◆ Why are people waiting for their drinks or food? Is there a hold-up in the kitchen? Or don't I have enough staff on duty?

◆ Why is the coffee from that very expensive coffee machine I so carefully sourced not being made or served properly? Do staff need more instruction on how to make good coffee?

◆ Are staff working as a team? In the kitchen? In the restaurant? As a whole?

Finally:

◆ How have staff handled the bills and their payment?

◆ Are staff saying goodbye in a pleasant manner? Are they sullen or smiling?

◆ Do customers look as if they have enjoyed being in your restaurant?

It is along list, but it is well worth taking the time and effort to go through these points and, if you find that some are justified and need action, address them.

Being a customer

Is the customer always right? No, of course not. We live in somewhat boorish times with some pretty unpleasant behaviour taking place in public places.

But, equally, there are many delightful human beings who will be charmed by your restaurant, your staff, your food and the ambience you have created. They are mostly the ones that will come to your restaurant

And, hopefully they will remember to:

◆ Turn up in time for a booking and respect your business, taking into account that the system of the restaurant (putting pressure on the kitchen) might suffer if they are late.
◆ Call the restaurant if they are going to be late.
◆ Contact the restaurant if numbers in their party are up or down as you can't magic chairs or tables out of thin air if the booking changes.
◆ Contact the restaurant to cancel a booking.
◆ Keep their drinking at a decent level and not get drunk on your premises.
◆ Complain politely if a problem occurs.
◆ Not treat staff as servants, but see them as professionals and equals.
◆ Not complain over trivia.
◆ Say thank you for good food and service which is music to staff's, chef's and management's ears.

Tips from established restaurateurs

◆ If starting, beware of your own naïvety.
◆ Select staff who wish to make catering their career rather than those just in it for the money.
◆ Don't select staff who have been through catering college and think they know everything. In this business you never stop learning.
◆ Treat your customers as you would good friends being guests in your own home.
◆ Be realistic and straightforward, avoiding all pretentiousness.
◆ Don't use your imagination just for the sake of seeming imaginative.
◆ Only cook what you understand and cook well.
◆ Buy in small quantities frequently so that your food is always fresh.

- If you mix a variety of ingredients from East and West, know what you are doing as it could result in a total mish-mash of flavours with customers running screaming from the premises. Pickled ginger with mashed potatoes doesn't work as a pairing.

- Get an accountant!

- A good review is worth thousands of pounds in advertising.

- Word of mouth is the best advertising. For every satisfied new customer, another five to ten people will hear of it from that customer.

- Be good humoured.

- Have good interpersonal skills.

- Have good feet!

- Be a mind reader.

- Honestly know your food and wine.

- Enjoy company and really like people.

- Hire staff carefully: they need to fit in personally as well as being efficient.

- Create a happy kitchen atmosphere. Don't have chefs who cook in anger. Customers will pick it up.

- The best food is soul food and you can't cook in chaos or that sweaty, macho, it's-hell-in-here-but-we'll-get-the-job-done atmosphere so beloved of catering regiments. Ever notice women don't cook like that?

- Cynicism and marketing always show. The best restaurants are expressions of the people who create them.

- Don't forget dining room improvement, service and menu improvement. Regular customers love to see the place they know and love, being maintained and improved.

- Believe in what you are doing and look at the long term.

- Be consistent.

- Raise your prices very slowly.

- Do not try to please everyone.

- Know your strengths and weaknesses.

- When starting your business keep your price below the competition and your quality above.

- It is important to be able to say 'no'.

- Develop your palate. Always try new tastes and keep up to date.

- Never serve food you do not taste.

- In good restaurants there are no VIPs. All your customers are VIPs.

- Being a restaurateur can eat up family life. Safeguard your family by delegating and spending more time with them. This is vital.

- Service is not servility.

- Encourage children to eat all types of food in your restaurant. They are the next generation of customers.

- It is a mistake to presume that good food alone makes for a good restaurant.

- Know your market and know who you are catering to, then design your menu, premises, ambience, pricing, service and style.

- Regard cooking and service as being of equal importance.

- Lead by example by training all staff to respect their work and the contribution they make to the restaurant.

- Avoid pushy advertising and salespeople.

- You need to be strong in mind and body, for restaurant demands are great.

- Be loyal to good suppliers and pay them on time. They will go out of their way to help you in the future.

- Never make drastic changes to the menu, but change it gradually and within seasons. Your customers might be put off by too drastic a menu change.

- Be patient with staff. You will rarely have perfect staff so look to their positive points and hope to improve their bad ones. See them blossom.

- Getting the right financial and accounting advice from the beginning is the difference between a viable and non-viable business.

- Keep up with your paperwork. If you can't, hire a book-keeper.

- Set up costs are frightening. Don't be put off. You have to spend money to make money.

- Kitchen equipment can be bought second-hand or leased.

- Market research is important. There is no point in offering your style of cooking or restaurant if there is no demand.

- It's a good idea to specialise, for example, specialise in organic, seafood or some other type of cuisine.

- Never rest on your laurels.

- Don't get one wine company to do your full list.

- Don't be under-financed as the pressure will force you to work all hours.

- Take good breaks to restore the brain and for inspiration.

- There are customers out there who are just out to give a restaurant a hard time. Grit your teeth and be so revoltingly pleasant they will be eating out of your hand.

- Attention to detail. It's the little things that matter.

- Staff must be constantly reminded, cajoled, kicked and generally encouraged to get it right.

- Don't chop and change your opening hours as it confuses people.

- Spread your bookings. The restaurant that allows all its customers to arrive at 8.30 pm is courting disaster.

- Happy bosses, happy staff, happy customers.

- Chefs should only become chefs when they develop their own skills: too many young chefs are influenced by fame and fortune and don't necessarily have the passion and heart.

- Despite everything, it is a most fascinating business.

- Ignore all the above if you're an accountant thinking of setting up a restaurant as an investment.

Should you decide to open a gastropub or brasserie I hope that the information, experiences and practicality – aided and abetted by common sense – in this book have helped you on your way to an informed decision.

If you have the desire to run your own place, make sure you have equal measures of pure passion coupled with a lot of knowledge and realism to start on the right foot.

May you open your business, and close it when you wish, not due to finances or poor business acumen – and may you have many valued customers who return for more and more of your rewarding hospitality.

But remember: change is the norm, not the exception. Keep ahead of the game.

I wish you good fortune.

Index